How To Start Your Own Improv Comedy Group

Paul Johan Stokstad

1st WORLD
LIBRARY
Literary Society

• Austin • Fairfield • Delhi

How To Start Your Own Improv Comedy Group

Paul Johan Stokstad

© 1st World Library – Literary Society, 2003
809 South 2nd Street
Fairfield, IA 52556
www.1stworldlibrary.org
First Edition

LCCN: 2003110590

ISBN: 1887472975

Readers interested in obtaining information
on 1stWorld Library: •Publishing Services
•Contributions •Book Conversion
• Convert-On-Demand / Print-On-Demand
contact www.1stworldlibrary.org

CONTENTS

This book is dedicated to Lali.
Thanks for saying yes.

Introduction

The goals of improv training

- ➤ Creating ensemble
- ➤ Releasing the power of the group
- ➤ Display connection
- ➤ Display commitment
- ➤ Comedy as a by-product
- ➤ Listening
- ➤ Physicality
- ➤ Stage awareness
- ➤ Live onstage capability
- ➤ Performer benefits
- ➤ Audience benefits

Creating Ensemble

Some things take time. Walking into a strange room full of strangers with a teacher that you've never met can be an intimidating experience. What we want as improv presenters is a group of performers that knows and trusts each other well, a group that is not afraid to fall on each other, be lifted into the air, or get tackled, hugged, or piled up in a jumble of limbs and bodies. You want a group that is completely friendly and trusting and open and safe with each other. Getting from complete strangers to a pile of puppies isn't something that happens overnight.

To start developing a team where each person knows each others capabilities, strengths, weaknesses, preferences, skill sets, and tendencies we use a number of workshop games that help develop trust and ensemble awareness, such as Trust Walk, Trust Fall, Lemmings, Give and Take, Stage Picture, Sneaky Movers, etc. These games break down physical shyness and begin building a visual and kinetic sense of the group as a whole.

Paul Johan Stokstad

Releasing the Power of the Group

You want people to experience the value of subsuming their individual needs for attention to the needs of the group. You want to get the shyer members to emerge in the warm glow of a safe environment, and get the assertive types to take it down a notch so that the power of the group can emerge. Often the most brilliant material is lurking just under the surface of that apparently shy girl. Often the show-off will find a great sense of relief in the group mind, since the only reason he was showing off before was because he felt responsible to make things entertaining for everyone.

Display Connection

We want the players to have a deep connection with each other. When they are playing the same games by the same rules under the same set of improv conventions, they automatically have a connection due to those agreed-on parameters. At the same time, the sense that they are alone onstage with no script, blocking, costumes or props causes us to emphasize the connectedness to an extreme degree. We have to maximize the connection in order to minimize the insecurity inherent in that situation.

Comedy as a By-Product

Improv is intrinsically funny. But there is a range of this quality, running all the way from riotously laughable on down to amusing and even just charming and surprising. You can have an improv scene where the performers are dead serious and the audience will be laughing uncontrollably. This is because there is always a serious commitment of the performer in comedy. But the situation is usually still laughable.

On the other hand, you can have a beautiful and poignant dramatic scene in an improv context, and it's a toss-up as to whether the audience will laugh or not. Sometimes the audience will laugh because they think improv is supposed to be funny. Sometimes they will laugh as a release of some emotion that they don't know what else to do with. It may be that what would normally be called humor will cross over into the realm of wonder, or even rich appreciation of some insight or improv virtuosity.

So, one thing that should be clear to you, as an improv presenter, is that the humorous element is not the goal of improv, anymore than getting applause is the goal of a basketball team. A basketball team is trying to get as many balls through the hoop as possible while minimizing the same sort of success for their opponents. The entertainment value is a by-product of that goal.

Entertainment will be what brings people to your shows, but it's the commitment of the players to accomplishing the tasks of the improv challenges that will fascinate and, as a by-product, amuse the audience.

So, it's improv, not improv comedy that is the subject of this book. Even so, you will probably get a few laughs along the way.

Paul Johan Stokstad

Listening

We are trying to get people to listen to each other. We want even the person who is speaking to be aware of the slightest move toward speaking by some other person. We would like someone who is loudly proclaiming an opinion to be able to hear someone start whispering behind him.

Most of all we need people to listen to each other, to give respect and focus to what the other person is saying. And of course we need people to learn to give and take, so that the performance doesn't degenerate into a shouting match or a jumble of people talking at the same time.

Fortunately there are workshop and performance games to develop this kind of sensitivity to each other, such as Give and Take, Party Tables, Flashback and Phone Bank.

These skills will become crucial when players get into the more adventurous and sophisticated long-form improv structures, since players can "edit" or stop one another's scenes, which can only happen if the active performers are waiting, open and listening for such an event

Physicality

In general we emphasize showing, not telling. We'd rather see someone sawing a log than have him say, "I guess I'll saw a log." Such storytelling is indicative of a low expectation of the audience. The other thing is that another player walking into the scene may not see a log being sawed, but rather an attempt to start a lawnmower, and offer to get some gas. If the first player is attached to his log-sawing scenario he will have difficulty saying yes to the "mistake" of the second player, and the scene will fall flat. Of course it was not a mistake, just an endowment or definition of the undefined physical motion of the first guy.

Another element of physicality is the power of physical contact onstage. The audience is completely isolated, sitting politely, trying not to bump each other. But onstage you can have people grabbing each other by the jaw and trying to look down each others throat, lifting some player in the air as an animal sacrifice, or hanging on each other like candies stuck together in the wash.

Such physical contact is magic onstage. I think this is partially due to the vicarious thrill that people have seeing somebody, anybody, in contact with another person. Contact requires tremendous trust, cooperation and agreement. Such connection is fresh and thrilling to the isolated viewer.

The other major value of physical contact is that we are not typically in contact with each other unless something extreme is happening. There are almost no situations that I can think of where two adult American males (for example) will be in contact, in public, other than with a handshake. Unless there is something wild going on: a wrestling match, two guys holding a rope with a hot air balloon on the other end, one guy teaching another how to walk after an accident, a sculptor chipping away at a block of stone, etc.

This means that, in improv, physical contact forces the performers to find some extreme situation to justify the contact. Hence the heightening of the intensity and, typically, the humor of the scene.

There is no way to hang out there alone onstage when someone is grabbing your leg and inspecting it for lice.

Physicality demands and forces commitment: show, don't tell. When in doubt, grab on.

Stage Awareness

We want our performers to be totally aware of what the other performers are doing onstage. If someone moves an arm upstage left we want the player downstage right to know it, register it, and respond appropriately, if necessary. We want the players to be sensitive to the movements of the entire group in addition to their own movements.

In addition, we need to acquaint new performers with the traditional stage awareness of sight lines and upstaging. The player needs to be aware that if they are standing at the back of the stage (upstage), the face of anyone addressing them will become functionally invisible to the audience. That means that they will be taking the focus of the audience's attention away from the other performer.

Taking focus is a valuable and welcomed move onstage in improv, as long as you are also willing to give focus, by, let's say, moving downstage when someone else is speaking.

We also need performers to be sensitive to an audience's desire to see their faces even when they are not speaking, and that may mean that if the improvised action of the scene that they are in brings someone between them and the audience, they will need to cheat out in one direction or another to bring their face back into view.

This is stage blocking on the fly, and improv performers need to practice and internalize such principles so that they naturally move onstage in ways that release the full power of the performance to the audience.

It's odd because we are busily playing a game, and you might think that the audience would become totally secondary, but if we don't consider the audience, at some point they will quit coming.

The way we deal with this is to make such considerations into general scene rules; i.e.- general rules that we use to guide every scene that we are in. Then they just become part of the game and, coincidentally, make things easier for everyone.

Live Onstage Capability

What we are hoping to develop is the ability to come onstage with nothing planned and generate material, develop characters and perform a believable scene. The games are wonderful, but overall, what we really want is the ability to create a scene, functionally from nothing. Scene from Nothing is the most obvious example of such a capability.

Such a capability distinguishes and improv performer from many actors, who often lives in fear of something going wrong, of forgetting lines, or having some prop in the wrong place. The latter incident is one of the funniest moments in the Comedy "Noises Off," where a prop has been moved and yet the inexperienced performer cannot alter her lines, much to the chagrin of the more alert performer.

The improv-trained actor should be able to do something, stay in character, and act appropriately until someone can right things and move on. Of course, a well-trained actor is so deeply sunk in character that she probably could do the same thing.

Even so, a sense of being in the moment and ready for anything is a hallmark of the improv player

Performer Benefits

The performer, therefore, benefits by gaining confidence in her ability to get up onstage with nothing planned. Since she can immediately engage in a number of projects, such as establishing a physical whereabouts, establishing an age and a body type, plus saying yes to any initiative from other players, she has a road map out of the wasteland.

The performer also of course gains the enjoyment of working with a group and of being amazingly creative onstage without a second thought about it. She is empowered, freed, and applauded. That's good.

Audience Benefits

The audience, of course, is entertained, and, in some ways, inspired. By seeing people working together with such confidence and commitment, the viewer breathes some of that value into their own life. By watching the magic of human creativity spontaneously burst out, the watcher is inspired to take more risks themselves. In any case, they can feel a bit more alive, watching something wonderful take shape before them. And then they can go take an improv class to get in on the real fun.

Chapter 1

Getting yourself going

- ➢ Who are you

- ➢ Where are you

- ➢ Getting it down

- ➢ Understanding your role

- ➢ What's in it for you

- ➢ One step ahead

- ➢ No Prima Donnas

Who Are You?

The question is, have you ever done improv before? If you are going to lead others in this onstage sport, it would be great if you have some improv experience. It's not obligatory, but you would do well, if you have never tried this stuff out, to get some friends or fellow teachers together and try out some of the games before you jump in to leading a group of improv rookies.

If you are an experienced improv performer, this book should give you a framework with which to structure training, rehearsals and performance. If you have a background in teaching or directing dramatic productions, you will have an advantage over people that have never put anything onstage, but you will have to put your usual toolset to one side for a while and learn some new skills and approaches.

If you do not plan to perform with your troupe you will have to keep learning to stay ahead of them. The ideal would be that you would be a sort of player/coach, in that you could be experiencing and playing right along with your people. But if that is not practical or appropriate for your situation. You can still go for it.

Where Are You?

Bear in mind that there will be many who think that there is no way you can do this. There are those who will laugh at the idea that this material can even be taught in a book. This is because, in Chicago, for example, you can take a year of improv classes for three hours a week and you are still considered a beginner.

On the other hand, I believe that you can do anything that you set your mind to. I'd like you to prove those doubters wrong, by studying this book carefully, reading other books on improv, too, and by trying things out with live volunteers.

I don't believe that you have to move to Chicago to do improv right. It's true that working on it that long will take you deep into the genre, and probably maximize your own performance potential. But we are not all going to move to Chicago. Some of us just want to get together with some friends and do a show once, or twice, or three hundred times. But not in Chicago, in Wausau, Wisconsin; Elizabeth City, North Carolina; Greeneville, Tennessee; Marianna, Florida; Rexburg, Idaho; and Odebolt, Iowa.

It would be good for you to go to Chicago to

see Improv Olympic (first choice) or Second City or Comedysportz. Or to Toronto to see Second City or Theatresports. Or San Francisco to see Bay Area Theatre Sports (B.A.T.S.). But you shouldn't think that just because you are not in a major city you can't practice, play, and perform improv.

They have great basketball in the big city. But just because there is a Michael Jordan in the world doesn't mean that you can't put up a hoop in the driveway and shoot nothing but net.

Improv is game play. Those that think you can only do it if you've been trained by them for two years have forgotten where improv came from: drama training for children. On the other hand, there is a lot to learn, and long-term training is great. If you have the money and live in Chicago, New York, L.A. etc. For the rest of us, we have books. Like this one.

Paul Johan Stokstad

Understanding Your Role

In founding and running an improv troupe you have to make some decisions about what kind of role you are playing. There are many potential aspects to it. You have to promote the idea of improv training. You will need to motivate people to train and to perform. You probably won't be able to pay anyone (maybe twenty people in Chicago get paid to do improv), so you'll have to inspire them. You need to balance out inflated and deflated egos in your troupe. You need to set schedules and performance times and venues. You'll probably have to do publicity, come up with posters, flyers, ads, Public Service Announcements, etc.

Tired yet? You'll have to learn to delegate.

The main thing to understand is:

What's in it for you?

Improv is all about empowering the group, about encouraging everyone that they are important members of the ensemble, and getting them to participate, without fear, in the group creation. As a teacher you are constantly trying to bring people out and give them more sense of empowerment. You are hoping to inspire them to participate fully as students and performers.

But you have to make sure that you save some of the fun for yourself.

You have to remember why you are doing this. Are you doing it to make money, or to do improv yourself? Is it to explore comedy as a producer or as an arts presenter? Or did you want to develop skit material using improv?

My goal was to gather a bunch of friends around me and to perform. But I did too much of the work and also eventually added a few people who made life miserable for me. Then, instead of just getting rid of the trouble makers I kept trying to win them over. Didn't work.

The point is that you need to be clear about

Paul Johan Stokstad

your own needs and make sure that they are getting met in addition to those of your troupe members.

One Step Ahead

The basic difference between the teacher and the student is that the teacher comes prepared and the student comes to be receptive. You only have to be one day ahead of your students. If you have done the readings and the planning, you should feel confident that you have something to offer the group. Don't let the fact that you are just learning the games yourself or experimenting with improv performance ideas eat away at your confidence. Everyone else just walked in. If you've done your homework, you are fully justified to give them some tasks of their own.

No Prima Donnas

Improv is not about creating stars. It's about creating ensemble. There is a great safety in that ensemble. Of course, there are always standouts on any team. But the individual standout will falter without the strength of the group. And even the "weakest" player makes a contribution and gains significantly by participation in the group effort. It's your job to balance out the egos and show people how the group coherence can both protect the weak and support the strong.

Sometimes the strong thing to do onstage is to wait quietly for the emergence of the "weak" player. The show-off can show maturity for once by staying silent and believing that the other person can carry the scene. Sometimes you'll be amazed at what comes out of the wallflower when you let her speak. Since she's been on the side of the action all this time, she has done a lot of watching and growing, and those roots go deep.

Chapter 2

Basic Agreements/Scene Rules

➤ Focus

➤ Give and take

➤ Say Yes

➤ Make Statements

➤ Make Contact

➤ Space Substance

➤ Stage Picture

Basketball is improvisational, but it's still practiced. You never know exactly what's going to happen when you get out on the basketball court, but you can practice skills that will help you once the ball starts moving.

Similarly, we never know exactly what is going to happen in an improv game or scene, but we can practice skills that will improve our chances of success.

In improv we have no lines, no blocking, no director, so we have to compensate by strengthening what we do have. What gets amplified to a maximum degree in successful improv is agreement. We agree with each other, we agree to play by the same rules. We agree that whatever the other person said is brilliant and important. We build on what they say. Since we have nothing to start with, we agree to build on anything that happens.

Basketball players practice dribbling, passing, shooting, defending, set plays, zone defenses, fast breaks, etc. By moving the ball around a lot between players, basketball teams tend to create scoring opportunities.

Improv players must also gain a set of skills to orient them in the playing environment, skills that translate into successful improv performances. Operating under this set of skills and agreements, they have a silent communication and connection that more than overcomes the lack of a script.

Focus

The first concept that the improv rookie needs to understand is the principle of FOCUS. We establish that every game has a focus (or even several). Some examples of game foci are:

➢ Playing a game as if you were a balloon filled with helium-
➢ Playing a scene where you constantly discover tiny objects in your environment
➢ Playing a game where each player can only say one word each at a time

In order to illustrate the concept of focus we usually start the first improv training session with a no focus game, in order to show what improv is not.

Most people have heard the anecdote that the fear of death ranks lower for most people than the fear of public speaking. People would rather die than stand up alone in public and give a speech. The real nightmare is, of course, to stand up in public to give a speech and have nothing to say. Standing there, swinging in the wind, just being watched.

So, that is what we do on day one to some hapless volunteer.

First we say, "What we are about to do is the most difficult thing that we will ever do," and ask for a volunteer.

When someone steps forward, we have them stand up, center stage. We say, "Stand there." They may say, "What should I do?" We say, "Just stand there."

Then we turn to the rest of the students, who are now sitting as an audience and we give them an assignment. We say, "Your job is to watch her, and observe what you see."

Usually several things will happen right away. The audience will giggle. The player onstage will giggle, or fidget, or ask another question.

You may have to remind them of their jobs. You can say: "Remember your job: watch her."

And then you watch her, too.

What you are waiting for are some signs of nervousness, some signs of self-consciousness. Some looking around, some shifting uneasily. The audience may also become uncomfortable for her.

Some people may not get nervous or fidgety. Usually this would be a born showman who loves and relishes the limelight. A rare bird. You may have to use several subjects to get the point across. Some people will actually get angry being asked to just stand there, exposed. Of course, they did volunteer.

Once the waiting has resulted in a few moments of nervousness or at least some coping mode visible in the behavior of the subject, you give them an instruction, such as, "Please count the number of seats in the room, loud enough so that all can hear you." If they finish counting you can have them start over. Other instructions could be anything, count the number of ceiling or floor tiles, etc.

Once they have engaged in the new behavior for about a minute, you stop them, thank them and have them sit down in the audience.

In the first situation your player had no focus, nothing to do. This is not how improv works. We are here dramatizing what should never happen to them again onstage. The second situation shows how improv works. You always have a focus, something that you are supposed to be doing onstage.

95% of the time the person with no focus will show signs of nervousness either physically or verbally. Their body will sometimes be rigid and posturally defensive. When we switch them to the focus on counting a noticeable change quickly emerges. Their body typically relaxes. Their voice acquires ease and even can become playful and entertaining.

Counting is an activity that any typical player can accomplish with ease. We give them something simple to do and they move into it with confidence.

At the end of this exercise we hammer

the point home by doing a post ludem analysis. I say post ludem instead of post mortem because post ludem means after the play, not after dying. I like it better, hope that you don't mind.

We explain that analysis of the focus exercise has six parts.

1. What she looked like in the first section
2. What she felt subjectively in the first section
3. How you felt watching her in the first section
4. What she looked like in the second section
5. What she felt subjectively in the second section
6. How you felt watching her in the second section

Usually the group will be able to note signs of nervousness in the volunteer in the first part and ease in the second. You also can direct people's attention to their own physical feelings of tightness or ease when the performer was under pressure or not. You then can explain how good improv works - the performer becomes natural, performs some easy task, and the audience relaxes.

We say, "This should never happen to you again." We clarify that improv always has a focus. Since the mind has something to focus on, it can happily follow those instructions and not be self-conscious. We engage the mind in some simple task, in effect disengaging it from self-analysis and self-consciousness.

This is the magical key to fearless improv performance onstage. You don't have time to get nervous. You're too busy!

Not that there isn't energy in the room with a live audience watching you, but when you take your focus off of yourself and put it onto the focus of, for example, coming up with the next word in a sentence being made up by two people, you successfully contribute to an entertaining scene that is being made up on the spot.

The entertainment value was not your goal. You only wanted to achieve your focus: the next word in the sentence. The situation is entertaining. You're not.

At this point we tell the students to always be aware of what their focus is when they go into a scene. If they feel themselves drifting off or slipping into laughter during a game or scene, usually they've lost focus.

I've lost the source of this quote, but it's famous: "Find the focus, it's the tail of the comet." Probably Keith Johnstone. The fact is that if you are not on focus, you are not going to feel any safer onstage than a basketball player who has forgotten which end of the court is which. Once he gets that straightened out, he'll know what to do.

The group agreement on focus sets the stage for all of improv. Unless everyone agrees on this element, players will not be playing the same game at the same time. One player will run with the ball while another will bounce it. One performer will be underwater while another is floating in outer space. Focus is a key improv concept.

There is another type of focus, i.e. – who has the focus of the audience's attention, and so these terms can get confused, but we can distinguish them by describing them as game focus versus stage focus.

Give and Take

You can make stage focus clear to new players with the several variations of the game Give and Take. First we start with Give. We get the group up out of the chairs that they sat in for the focus analysis. We tell them that we hope they enjoyed their last moments in the audience, because now they are all players.

We introduce the concept of making gibberish sounds, i.e. - nonsense syllables spoken out loud. We have them all practice that for a few moments.

We explain the concept of "**share your voice**" which means that we expect them to speak loud enough so that the farthest person away from them in the group can hear them. We explain that this is the first of many stage behaviors that they will turn into habits, because sharing your voice onstage will someday mean sharing it with the last person in the last row in the theatre.

We explain **side coaching**, which means that you as the facilitator will occasionally say things during an exercise, which they are to incorporate into their play without stopping to ask questions. So, for example, during the next exercise you may say, "share your voice" if you feel that they are not speaking gibberish loud enough to be heard.

To start the Give exercise we explain that we will have them mill around on stage in a loose flow of bodies passing by each other in random patterns and then you will say "freeze," after which they are to assume a "soft" freeze in the position that they were in when they heard the side-coached command of "freeze."

A soft freeze means that they hold their position but don't strain at it. We don't want them looking and moving about during the exercise, because that will take stage focus from the person who is moving about.

After they freeze (you explain), one of them will start moving about the stage speaking in gibberish, gesturing as necessary in that imaginary speech, and then that person will walk up to one of the frozen players and clearly give the focus to that person by addressing them directly in gibberish, gesturing and then stopping all sound and action, assuming a soft freeze of their own.

It should be clear to the new player that he or she now has the onstage focus, and that they are to move about the stage speaking in their own private gibberish until they, too give the focus to some other player. And so it continues through the entire group.

If you have a large group you will probably do well to break it down into groups of four to six for most of these exercises.

The value of this exercise is to give performers

an awareness of who has the onstage focus at any particular time. By letting that person carry the scene for that moment and not muddying up the overall stage picture with distracting activities that take focus from the key player, the experienced player allows the scene to stay focused and powerful.

The next version of this game is Give and Take, which starts the same way but no one gives the focus away until someone takes it. The focus is taken from the strolling gibberizer by some new player who starts an action and a new round of gibberish. What that does is signal the old player to stop speaking gibberish, stop moving, and enter a soft freeze. Then the new player takes over.

You should note that there is no taking without giving. If a new player opts to start moving and speaking and the original player doesn't freeze out, there will be two foci onstage and the scene will start to muddy.

It is the agreement that when a new person comes in the old one will fade out that makes onstage improv ensemble performance work. The onstage focus can move from player to player, but unless there is tremendous respect and cooperation among the players, it will be a mess.

We can take a moment and bring out some stage presentation principles here, explaining how focus is given and taken, i.e. – how you can give onstage focus to someone else by moving closer to the audience (downstage) and looking back upstage to the speaker. This is a generous act that the skilled player uses to give the overall scene focus at the expense of his or her own temporary visual fame.

Having played Give and Take, it passes into the vocabulary of side coaching, where it has the effect of reminding people to share verbally and physically onstage.

Say Yes

This is a core principle of most improv performance, and although there are situations where forms of "no" may be okay, in general the "Say Yes" dictum still holds weight.

In improv we don't have prepared lines to say, we don't have staging instructions, or even any props, usually. In a scene we may have been given a relationship and a location for two players onstage, but that's it, except for the focus that we are going to apply to those given elements.

Even so, we need as many tools to get something going as we can. The Say Yes principle gives us an easier road to creating a scene from virtually nothing.

This is where improv leaves the real world behind.

If a man walks up to a woman that he hardly knows and asks her out on a date, she will in all likelihood say no. That's the real world. If that happens onstage the scene is dead and someone has to do something new to bring it to life again. The logical thing is for the guy to argue with the woman, for her to resist, and thereby the scene can die many times in a row, while the players and the audience die of embarrassment all around.

I know because this happened in one of my first improv workshops. I made the players go back and run the scene again but saying yes to the date question, and the scene came to life with decisions about where to go and what to do.

One game that begins training players in this skill is sometimes called **Ad Agency.** Another name for it is **Yes And...** The way that this works is that you gather the players around an imaginary table where you place an imaginary object to which you assign an arbitrary, made-up nonsense name such as (for example), "the Gibby."

Since we are pretending to be ad agency executives, artists and writers standing around a table with a new product that we have to market and sell, we come up with ideas as to how we could sell it and exclaim to each other about the cool features it has.

Someone starts the conversation out by saying something like, "well, the Gibby is the coolest shade of blue, I think it is very distinctive, and it will appeal to women of all ages." Then the next person agrees strongly with that statement and builds on it by saying, "Yes, and we could probably get probably get every woman in the U.S. to buy one, and even name their children after it." The next person may say something new, such as, "Yes and I think the fact that it has that sticky quality will mean that storage will be a snap, since you can stick it onto anything without leaving a stain."

You'll note that the exercise has the requirement that each new contributor say the phrase "yes and..." before their statements. This forces them to agree with what the other person says.

This is a good habit to start developing onstage. If I say, "my blue parrot has mononucleosis" and you say "What blue parrot?" or "That's not a parrot, it's a potato," you have killed the baby scene that I just started. If I say the same thing and you say "Yes, and I believe that they get it from pecking their partner's toes, not from kissing," we all of a sudden have a scene where we can rue the increase in toe-pecking parrots, and we also will probably soon have an audience surfing around in waves of laughter.

Having established this practice, we can then graduate the term "Say Yes" to side-coaching status, and use it to culture the habit to agree with what others give us onstage.

Of course, it's not enough to just say yes. You have to add something to the game. What works here is to consider that what was just said as the most brilliant possible idea that anyone could have had. So we say yes and then build on the previous statement. So, it's yes and BUILD. We can emphasize that and even make a game of it. And we do.

Knowing that whatever I say will be welcomed, exclaimed upon and embellished makes venturing forth into the unknown a safer move. By doing this we create a safe environment for new material to emerge. We also can end up in some fairly unusual spaces such as my response to one person's decision to shoot me onstage that that it would be fine but would he please shoot me in the leg and in the shoulder this time because I'd never been shot there before.

If I would have said no, the scene would have died and I would have been shot anyway. Say yes, and you may die, but the scene will live on. In that scene, I came back as a ghost and complimented his shooting.

Make Statements

Other than by saying no, the other quick way that you can kill a scene is by asking questions. No rule should be unyielding, but in general a question adds little or nothing to a scene.

Asking a question is like passing around the onstage focus like a hot potato, saying, "you take it, I don't want it." The slow death of the scene accelerates when the only possible response to the question is a yes or no. For example, the following scene:

Q – How old are you?
A – Six
Q – Do you come here often?
A – Yes
Q – What is your name?
A – Sally

As opposed to this scene:

Statement: You look like you are about six years old

Statement: Yes, I'm six but I do have a driver's license

Statement: Oh, yes, one of those young genius licenses, cool.

Statement: Yes, and the nice thing is that your speed limit is automatically the same as your IQ.

Statement: Wow, so I suppose you'd have to have a Lamborghini to break the law!

Statement: We're talking a Saturn rocket

Statement: Golly, I'd like to go Saturday night drag racing with you!

Statement: Well, you could but I can't stay up that late, I'm only six.

The second scene starts with a perfect example of what is known as an endowment. The first speaker endows the other with an age. The second accepts the endowment and builds on it. Notice how the second scene builds because each speaker agrees with the previous statement and then adds their own.

A statement is a gift or even an endowment. A question is a side-stepping motion that adds nothing to the scene and can even leave your co-player out there alone, dangling in the headlights of the audience's concern about where the scene is going.

One way to develop a statement or endowment habit onstage is to play a simple game called **Three Statements.**

To do Three Statements you form the workshop group into two lines. It works best if the lines don't have equal numbers in them so that the pairings vary.

The first person in line A faces the first person in line B. The other members of each line are standing in line behind the first people. The two first people step out to face each other and one makes a statement. Then the other makes a statement, usually something about the first statement. Then back to a statement by the first. That's it. After three statements have been made the first players rotate to the back of the line, and the next players step up.

You'll be amazed at how hard it can be for people to simply make statements rather than ask questions. This exercise cultivates the gift-giving statement habit.

This phrase "make statements" becomes a positive side-coaching term that is preferable to saying "no questions." If we emphasize the gift-giving behavior of making statements, the scene-wearying questions go away on their own.

Make Contact

Even a casual study of human interaction should be able to come up with the observation that we don't look at each other in the eyes very often, at least not for very long. We check in, we glance, and look away. Certainly in a major city in the U.S. you will almost never get eye contact on the street. In prison it could get you in serious trouble to even look at anyone.

But when people want to convey something important, they will look straight at you. Long moments of intense gazing into the eyes are characteristic of only two groups, i.e. - lovers and optometrists.

Knowing this, we use eye (and physical) contact to add to the intensity and focus onstage.

To dramatize this to a new group of improv players I ask for a volunteer, a location, and a relationship between us, and then run a short scene of 3-4 lines, and then stop. Then I re-run it with new instructions to my partner, and then re-run it again with another layer of instructions. Then I ask the audience (students) to rank the three scenes in terms of their dramatic interest, and 95% of the time they will rank the last scene first, the second scene second, and the first scene last.

Then I tell them what I told my partner, explaining that in the first scene I didn't tell my partner anything. In the second scene I privately instructed my volunteer that he could not speak to me unless he looked at me in the eyes, and he could not refer to an object unless he looked at that object. In the third scene I told my partner that they couldn't speak unless they are physically in contact with me, and vice versa.

What the second assignment does is instantly create connection between us. People only look at each other in the eyes when something important is happening, and so somehow our second scene automatically seems to acquire intensity and importance. And people never touch each other unless something really important is happening, and so somehow the intensity goes up another entire notch.

Here is a sample of such a progression:

I pick a kid named Fred out of the group. The group (I'm making this up as I go) tells us that we are in a zoo. I ask where in the zoo. They say at the cotton candy counter. I ask for a relationship, they say that we are uncle and nephew. Fine, I say, and start the scene:

Me: Wow, that's a really wild color of cotton candy
Fred: Yeah, it looks like Don King's hair on Acid
Me: Yeah, I guess we should have some.
Fred: Okay, but you hold the leopard
Me: Alrighty.

That's the first run.

The second run goes like this

Me: Wow, that's a really wild color of cotton candy (I say, grabbing the imaginary cotton candy and stretching it out like taffy)
Fred: Yeah, it looks like Don King's hair on Acid (He says, grabbing it out of my hands and looking straight in my eyes)
Me: Yeah, I guess we should have some. (I say, staring back at him)
Fred: Okay, but you hold the leopard (He says, reaching down to pick up the leopard)
Me: Alrighty. (I say, holding up the leopard, looking at it and then looking at Fred)

That's the second run. Then comes try #3:

Me: Wow, that's a really wild color of cotton candy (I say, grabbing onto Fred and cowering behind him)
Fred: Yeah, it looks like Don King's hair on Acid (He says, pushing me to the front)
Me: Yeah, I guess we should have some. (I say, hanging on and staring at him in fear but with determination)
Fred: Okay, but you hold the leopard (He looks down, grabs and hands me the leopard)
Me: Alrighty. (I take the leopard and hold it up toward the cotton candy like a weapon while I help push him forward with my body as we both creep slowly forward to grab a bit of cotton candy)

The third run is inevitably the most vivid, powerful, compelling and hilarious to the audience. Not that hilarity is what we are shooting for, but it is often an audience result when you make physical contact. It's not that physical contact is intrinsically funny. It's due to the fact that we as performers have to go to extremes in order to justify the physical contact. If things have to be intense to have sustained eye contact, they have to be even more extreme to have physical contact.

My theory is that this is exactly what audiences come to the theatre, to the ballpark, and the movies to see: connection. People like to see people connecting, working together, moving together, and solving problems together. I explain that the audience is completely disconnected, sitting there, trying not to bump each other or invade each other's space, and yet they love it when the performers are connected, looking deep and long at each other, grabbing on for dear life.

A group of rookie performers will stand on stage and try to say lines without looking at each other, without even acknowledging each other. The audience feels no connection and starts to lose interest. In improv rehearsals we can side coach "Make Contact," which means connect with the imaginary objects that you use and connect with each other by looking at and grabbing onto each other. When performers do this, the audience is thrilled with the power of that connection.

When a scene is dying I usually grab onto somebody. Usually the scene is resuscitated. But if not, at least we all fall together.

Space Substance

Viola Spolin refers to imaginary three-dimensional space and objects as being made up of "space substance." Making connection with imaginary objects onstage is easier if you give them more reality. Imaginary objects become imbued with reality when you give them a heightened degree of attention.

The way we train for this is as follows:

We stand the group of players in a circle, facing inward. We say, "Consider that we are going to reach out into the space between us and find an object made out of space substance. This substance will have weight and shape. You will find an object, and then examine it in your hands." Once they all do that, you say, "Now place the object on a shelf behind you." Then you have them repeat the exercise once or twice more.

The emphasis here is on finding objects, not on creating them. If we create an object it comes out of our intellect. But if "find" the object it acquires more external reality both for the player and the audience. When a player finds an object, looks at it, inspects it a bit, and then uses it, the object acquires a high degree of believability for an audience.

Beginning performers will pick up an imaginary pencil and yet when you look closely their fingertips are in contact as if nothing was there. Experienced space object users will look at the pencil before picking it up, maybe examine it a bit, use it, and then feel compelled to put it down someplace before going on with the scene.

You can mime these two versions of "pencil" for your players to clarify the difference, and then ask for their observations.

There are many other games dealing with objects, including warm-up and performance games. But this will get your people started.

Stage Picture

Along with working on improv we give our people a quick introduction to stage performance principles. I mentioned the "share your voice" precept earlier. We also we want them to share their face(s).

Stage picture awareness requires that each player's face be seen by every audience member whenever possible. To do this in the midst of action each performer may have to make little adjustments in where they stand or look.

To train for this we have the group mill about aimlessly in a fairly tight group and then say, "freeze. " We then say "stage picture" at which time each player is required to make one smooth move to a position where she can see every (empty, this is a rehearsal) chair in the audience area. We do this several times, and in the later iterations ask them to find levels, i.e. - find a final position where some of them are high, some are at the middle level and some low to the ground.

Doing this exercise creates an interesting series of tableaux of the entire group, and trains the players to begin to perceive how the whole group looks on stage.

Paul Johan Stokstad

People are fascinated with other people's faces. They want to see your face onstage. If you are hidden behind someone else they will get frustrated. The "stage picture" habit and side-coached instruction breaks up the sight lines and brings those lovely faces out to satisfy the audience's curiosity.

These general points are fundamental to the group's understanding of what we are doing onstage together. The first few workshops have to clarify and stabilize these skills so that all players are playing from the same level of commitment and understanding. Then you can really play together.

This chapter concerns basic agreements and/or scene rules. We consider these basic agreements because unless your players all understand them they will not be playing the same games with each other onstage. And they certainly won't understand the side coaching. We consider these items to have the status of scene rules because they are the basic rules that allow scenes to work.

In improv performances we often use improvisational games that stimulate player creativity in order to accomplish the tasks of the game. The audience is tickled by the players' creativity, even if the audience doesn't know what the rules of the game(s) are. In the midst of these games we almost always end up in some kind of human interaction or scene that the players must dramatize.

What happens is that the game rules can get you into and out of a scene, but the scene rules always apply in addition to the game rules. The scene rules keep the scenes full of energy and purpose. The games just serve as vehicles to make the scenes happen. So, your players need to live and breathe the basic agreements of the scene rules, so that they can function properly when the real play begins.

Chapter 3

Understanding Games

- ➤ What games do

- ➤ The underlying scenework

- ➤ How many balls in the air?

- ➤ Game focus evaluation

- ➤ Scene rules evaluation

- ➤ Personal evaluation

- ➤ Entertainment evaluation

- ➤ The role of the audience

What games do

A game is a simplified world. There are clear guidelines. There are boundaries. There are tasks to perform and positive feedback to be had simply for trying to achieve those goals.

Everything is clear-cut, unlike most of life.

What theatre games do is occupy the mind while training the individual in a number of presentation skills. Any particular game may emphasize one or another presentation skill. If we play a mirror game we are learning to watch other people onstage, and to physically duplicate that behavior. The growth of mind-body integration is obvious. If we play a game where two players are dubbing the voices of two other players, you train the physicality of the non-verbal players and the quickness and observation powers of the second group, plus increasing cooperation among all.

But the main value is the freedom that game playing brings to the player. They improv player gets absorbed in the game challenge and is no longer worried about the audience. This turned Viola Spolin's shy children into assertive theatrical performers, because it was all (presented as) a game.

The underlying scenework

Onstage games almost always involve some kind of scenework. It's analogous to a track meet where the athletes' overall strength, flexibility, endurance and cardiovascular efficiency provide a basis for all the running, jumping and throwing events.

The games are really just vehicles to get the players in and out of scenes. It's important that your players feel totally at home in doing scenes so that they are at ease when the game lands them there.

The workshop games tend to develop scene skills, such as group agreement, give and take, stage picture, saying yes, making statements, etc. If the players remember these things when they are onstage, you will have good scenes and good games and a good time will be had by all.

How Many Balls in The Air?

It would not be unlikely for a particular player in an improv game to be trying to give reality to an imaginary pencil while moving with the body image of a stork with a legato (fluid, smooth) internal rhythm in a floating imaginary atmosphere while constantly searching for tiny imaginary objects while playing the role of a bed bug stuck on a piece of toe jam on an Australian aborigine.

That may seem like a lot to be carrying around, but most of it would just be starting points from which a certain physicality and bits of onstage business would result.

Let's unpack the situation where such a pile of elements could be carried around by one person. First of all, giving reality to imaginary objects is a fundamental skill in an environment where we typically have no props. Looking at and playing with the prop in a studied way can give a greater sense of reality to the object. This is object work which needs to become second nature to an improv player, so, since it is automatic to our imaginary skilled player, let's cross it off the list of balls in the air.

When the player is waiting for her scene assignment, or just after it begins she may decide to take on the body image of a stork, and the floating atmosphere. This is an instant way into creating a physicality that translates into a particular kind of movement. Once she has made this choice she is in it, and it should take little attention to keep it going if she has a history of doing animal/people work.

The game itself may be **Tiny Objects**, which requires a player to constantly discover tiny objects in her environment, so, since that's the main focus of the game, it shouldn't be too difficult to continue. The toe jam location and the bed bug persona was probably given by an audience member, and that is simply who she is.

Let's say our player is Louise and that she has a partner named George, who has decided to have the body/movement image of a whale (even though he is a bed bug), also in a floating atmosphere, and he is playing the same tiny objects game.

The scene might go like this:

Louise: George, darling, I believe that we are in some unusual feeding grounds [flicking some dust off of her clothing]
George: Yes, precious, I believe that we have arrived in a rather gooey state. [Leaning over slowly and picking up a bit of goo to eat].
Louise: I suppose that we should add it to the list.
George: Oh yes, the list of putrid dining spots.
Louise: Quite. I do believe it will be a best seller [pulling out her pencil and inspecting it for sharpness].
George: So, I suppose you'll be needing the back, then

[licking some residue off of his fingers as he turns his back for her to write on].

Louise: Yes, indeed [pushing him to the ground and sitting on his behind]

George: I love this part [laying on his stomach, picking up tiny morsels and popping them into his mouth as he kicks his feet playfully in the air behind Louise]

Louise: I know you do, darling, I know you do [starting to write on his back]. (BLACKOUT)

That is a perfectly believable improv scene, with physicality, bits of business, and characters that emerged out of choices of atmosphere and animal archetypes. The primary game was the tiny objects assignment. But there's nothing stopping a skilled improviser from adding a few more elements at the onset to give the scene more texture.

In most improv games, however, there are one or two major game goals under focus, with the whole set of guidelines for scenework as an underlying framework. You'll notice that the aspects of the Australian Aborigine, the floating atmosphere and the legato quality have hardly any effect on the story. The latter may have given rise to the slightly effete, upper society dialogue. And the aborigine element might come into play later. It doesn't really matter that all the elements get woven into the scene. They are a point of departure for what is really happening, i.e.- a scene in which a believable relationship can be explored, in character, where dialogue that is appropriate for the situation can emerge with minimum effort.

Game focus evaluation

If you are leading an improv group you will have to guide the players in what constitutes good improv. Beginning players will often complain that what they did wasn't funny. Extroverts without an improv background may be searching to find some joke that they can insert to make it funny, to get attention, or to "carry " the scene for all of the shy people.

It's your job to explain what we are really looking for. The first question is, did we fulfill the demands of the game?

The game may be something like **Phone Bank**. In Phone Bank individual players enter, at different times, a space with an imaginary row of phones such as you might find at an airport. Each player picks up a phone, dials a number, and starts talking. When one player starts to talk, the other players reduce the sound of their conversations to a whisper. Any player can retake the focus by bringing up the sound of their conversation, at which time the previous speaker will fade out. Players keep going with their conversations, chronologically, even when the audience does not hear them. Then, one by one, the players re-take focus, make final comments, hang up, and leave the stage.

This game, when done properly, can create a fascinating collage of character types passing each other in a public place, having their little moment on the phone, and then leaving the space empty.

Evaluating the success of the game would include mean asking if everyone understood what they were supposed to do, whether they faded out effectively when the next person spoke, whether they continued their conversation believably, and got off stage within an effective period of time.

Paul Johan Stokstad

Scene rules evaluation

The same scene, considered from the perspective of scene rules, takes on another flavor. Of course, the Give and Take structure of the game is a fundamental scene rule, and so that analysis is relevant in both environments. But there are also considerations of object work, in believably dialing and holding the phone, opening doors, if any, on the phone booths, and putting the phone handset back in the same place you picked it up. There are also considerations of volume that side-coaching statements such as Share Your Voice are designed to address. This is just a start.

Personal evaluation

You also want your players to be able to evaluate how they felt doing the scene. We are, after all, hoping that this will be "play" for the players. We want them to feel that their experience of the game is important. Were the game rules clear to them? Did they retain their focus or get lost in the presence of an audience? Hopefully the comfortable familiarity of being on the phone gave them something secure to hold onto onstage.

Entertainment evaluation

Finally we evaluate how entertaining we thought the piece was. It may seem surprising that I put this one last, but it is intentional. Not that we don't care about the entertainment value. Just that if we do the first three things properly the fourth will typically come along. The games are intrinsically interesting. Most people would be fascinated to hear other people's phone conversations, even if they are imaginary. So if you play the game right, creating a believable scene, and you seem to be having fun, the audience will be right with you, listening in.

Evaluation can take place in a workshop setting, or even post-performance. Ideally post-performance evaluation will take place with a video replay, if time allows.

By establishing these guidelines for evaluation, we redirect the attention of the new player to where it belongs, on the technical elements of onstage games and scenework, and on their own enjoyment. Letting go of the worrying about entertainment value puts the focus on the elements that will create the entertainment value. The less they worry about how they look, the better they look. It's a great load off of the player, and a win-win for their future audience(s).

The Role of the Audience

The audience, therefore, is a secondary consideration for the improv player, just as the sports audience is not (usually) part of the game in a sporting event. The audience's attention adds excitement to the event, but their entertainment is a by-product of the improv activity.

We do ask the audience for suggestions for our improv games, such as settings, occupations, relationships, etc., but that is to a large degree only to help assure them that the material that they are seeing is truly improvised and not planned. We could just as easily make up these elements ourselves, and indeed, in games such as Scene from Nothing (see Appendix B), we do that very thing.

It's interesting to note the types of suggestions that we solicit from the audience, since the topic illuminates some fundamental principles of improv and some practicalities of improv performance.

Viola Spolin described three aspects that need to be decided onstage, i.e. - who, what and where. We need to know who the players in a scene are, where they are and what they are doing.

When we solicit a "where" we are looking for a

location, which I narrowly define as a location that will fit on the stage. This is a crucial distinction when getting suggestions from a live audience. When asked for a location for two performers in an upcoming game, audience members will sometimes make suggestions such as "France" or "New York City." At that point the emcee must ask for clarification, by saying something like "Where in France?" until there is a suggestion that is specific enough to fit onstage, such as, on the observation deck on the top of the Eiffel Tower.

This is mandated because we want the players to be able to find and use physical specifics of a believable environment. Of course, it is possible to run a scene where France would fit on the stage, but then the players would have to be enormous giants and it would be very destructive to the French landscape, which could be interesting, at least. Still, for most scenes we want a specific, localized "where."

When we speak of "who" we are generally looking of a relationship, e.g. - co-workers or blood relations, such as father/daughter, brother/sister, etc. Soliciting a relationship tends to bring elements of relative status into the scene, which were explored in depth by Keith Johnstone's *Impro* and continue to form the basis of games such as Status Switch. In any case such suggestions get the ball rolling and the scene players can pick it up and run with it.

What we don't really want from an audience is the "what" of the scene, i.e. - what are they doing. Sometimes an audience member will spontaneously suggest something like "they are getting married," or "she's dumping him." If we give the players the who, what and where of the upcoming scene, they will have nothing to do other than recreate the audience's suggestions. We don't want that. We want them to discover something new, surprising and fresh without any real prompting.

In some ways we don't really care what the audience comes up with, other than as a starting point. The suggestions just give a set of initial conditions, and the players move into the new and surprise everyone, themselves included.

Chapter 4

Workshop #1: Basic Agreements

With a new group of players we need to establish some ground rules, clarify what improv is, break down some shyness and begin to establish a sense of trust among the players. A performing group has to have a great deal of trust and cooperation and even a deep ease with physical contact in order to function effectively onstage. A beginning workshop gives a taste of these values.

It may be good to start with some simple warm-ups to get things going. These get people involved and can be used at the beginning of every session. They also will double as warm-ups for actual performance nights, engaging players in a familiar activity that settles jitters and orients them toward working together.

You can start with **Ooga-Booga.** You can call it whatever you want, but that's my name for it. In this game the players stand in a circle, facing inward, and one player starts the action by making a nonsense sound (such as **Ooga-booga**) and a clear physical movement or gesture, clearly throwing the gesture toward some other person in the circle. That person repeats the sound and the gesture back to the sender, and then turns and makes a new nonsense/gibberish sound and a new gesture to someone else in the group.

You continue this until all members have been active at least once. What you want people to do is to react quickly and without thinking, passing the focus around the group. You ask them to tighten up the circle and speed up the exchange.

Freed up from the need to say something meaningful, they gain the habit of making a quick response when the focus is thrown their way, rather than trying to be clever or funny. They learn to just react, not act.

The next warm-up I call **Inka-Pink**. This is also done standing in a circle. One player starts the exercise by making a gesture and a sound, such as "inka-pink." Everyone in the circle then copies both the sound and the physical gesture. Then the person on the left of the first person changes the sound and the gesture, and the whole group follows suit. And so it continues around the circle until all have made the change. We then modify this same exercise so that anyone in the circle can change the sound and the gesture. This begins to train the group to watch, listen and respond to input from any and all players.

A good thing to do next is to work on building trust. A basic trust game is the **trust fall**. Trust fall is done with four or five players standing around a single player who closes their eyes and, keeping their body straight, begins to fall toward the outer circle of players, where they are caught and brought back to a vertical position. We let each player fall a few times and then rotate through the entire group. We emphasize protecting the player, that as many people as it takes to support the player should all pitch in at the same time as we protect the player from falling.

Then we do a **blind trust walk**, which involves having pairs of players lead each other around the room, first one and then the other player closing their eyes. The guiding player takes responsibility for protecting the "blind" player from obstacles, plus helping them explore the environment, touch objects with intriguing textures, etc.

After this we can do a bit of evaluation. We ask what it felt like to lead and to be led. We ask if they noticed new things with other senses than the visual, or moved differently when blind. Usually some people will have insights or experiences to share. In exercises like this we are not only expanding their sense of trust, we are also getting them into a habit of observing their environment in a new way, of using new senses, or using them differently.

Another useful game at this point is the **mirror** game.

In mirror two lines face each other, and you give each line a name, such as A and B. You have a player from each line pair up and face one member of the opposing line. Then you explain that line B is to mirror the movements of line A exactly, including all leg, torso, arm, and even facial movements. You have them do that for a while. Then you stop them (I say "come to rest"). Then you have them switch roles, with line B leading.

Then you say, "this time B will start and when I say switch, A will take over, and then again I will say switch and B will lead again, and so on."

After that has gone on for a minute or so, you stop them and give the final version, which is that one group will start leading and that at some point, with no signal from you, the other party will take over, and then again with no signal, the original party will begin leading again, and so on.

You let them do that for a while, and then say, "When you have made three switches, sit down."

When all have become seated you can evaluate. You ask what it was like to do this exercise. What you are hoping for is that some people may have experienced a sense that they didn't know at some times who was leading and who was following. Viola Spolin calls this "following the follower." What that experience indicates is that a high degree of communication and connection has started to happen between those two players.

This type of intuitive connection is the beginning of what you are hoping will develop onstage between all of your players at all times.

At this point you have probably done enough to get people somewhat familiar with each other, and it's time to introduce some of the improv fundamentals that we discussed earlier.

So this is where you can run **the Focus, Give and Take, Say Yes, Make Statements, Make Contact, Space Substance, and Stage Picture** exercises that we described in Chapter 2.

In this first session we try to briefly introduce effective improv evaluation procedures. We de-emphasize entertainment as a goal and put the focus on the process. We evaluate whether the game was played properly, according to its rules. We evaluate whether "scene rules" of give and take, and "say yes" were upheld. We look at presentation factors such as stage picture and "share your voice." Finally we consider the entertainment value.

By looking at all of these elements of performance rather than simply evaluating the entertainment value, we put the performers attention on the pieces that when assembled together help create the entertainment value.

An experienced improv performer will not be primarily oriented toward the audience's entertainment any more than a professional athlete can be primarily concerned about crowd applause. What the athlete and the improv veteran are seeking is excellence, the experience of doing their personal best, playing with a group of excellent peers.

The audience's appreciation of that excellence is a by-product or after-effect. The greatest joy is in doing well, in being in the middle of it all, and the audience just witnesses it.

This is an example of the self-absorption of the improv experience. The player is so busy with the assigned tasks of the game, with scene rules, with supporting her fellow players, etc. that she doesn't have time to worry about the audience. Which is exactly analogous to the experience of participation in a team sport.

By putting the new player's attention on themselves and on the technical aspects of improv play, we wean them away from worrying about the audience, which quickly lessens their fear of performance.

This is a lot of material to cover on Day 1, but if there is still time, you might give them a treat by having them do one performance game, such as Gemini or Mr. Know It All (see appendix).

Summary of Day One Activities:

- Ooga-Booga
- Inka-Pink
- Trust fall
- Blind Trust walk
- Mirror game
- Focus
- Give and Take
- Say Yes
- Make Statements
- Make Contact

- Space Substance
- Stage Picture
- Evaluation procedures

Game List: (see appendix B)

- Gemini
- Mr. Know It All

Chapter 5

Workshop #2: Exploring the Group/Space

On day two we want to continue establishing the concepts that we worked on in day one and introduce some more tools such as considerations of Imaginary Rhythms and Atmospheres. We may also be able to get to Time of Day/Occupation/Age games today. All of these games start developing a set of character-building tools that players can instantly call on when they enter a scene.

We start again with warm-ups, Ooga-Booga, Inka-Pink, and then some Mirror work. It wouldn't hurt to review Give, and then Give and Take.

A fun variation on the regular Mirror game is **Three-peat**, where there is one main player and three "modelers." The way this game works is to have three "modeler" players line up, one behind each other. The main player stands facing the first modeler in line. The first modeler sits on the floor and restricts their activities to facial gestures, the second modeler kneels and does arm and hand motions, while the third modeler remains standing and does leg/foot movements.

The main player tries to mirror the face of the first modeler, the arms of the second and the legs of the third. This requires a tremendous degree of multi-tasking and observational skills, and in addition is typically hilarious to watch and to do. The players rotate through every position.

Another valuable warm-up to introduce at this point is **Story Circle**, which develops verbal quickness without encouraging cleverness or clowning. Story Circle is simply the whole group standing in a circle, facing inward, and telling a story, one word at a time. Anyone can start the story.

Imaginary Rhythms and **Atmospheres** work together, so you can introduce them as a unit. Again you arrange the group in a circle, and you explain that you are going to give them a series of instructions to follow while they walk around in the circle. First you introduce the concept of imaginary atmospheres, by having them walk imagining that they are floating, buoyed up by the atmosphere. Then you tell them to bring their walk back to normal.

Then you ask them to try "molding," which you can explain as like walking through a thick liquid substance like molasses. As they try this you should look for total body involvement. They entire body should seem to be pushing through the substance, not just the hands. You can side-coach, "feel it with your whole body." Then back to normal.

Finally you have them try "soaring," which is similar to floating but more dynamic. The idea is that they are as if soaring through the sky or outer space.

Then we add the element of rhythms. You introduce the concept of staccato physical movement by demonstrating movement that happens only in jerks, or discrete, separate units. Then you have them try to move that way, walking around the circle. That won't take long; so then you introduce the opposite rhythmic style, which is legato, i.e. - smooth, unbroken, flowing movement.

Having done all this we then ask them to try two at once, specifying, for example, legato/floating as the first pair. Then you might try staccato/molding. Then you continue mixing it up with staccato/floating, or legato/molding, etc.

As you do these final exercises you might stop between and ask them to suggest characters that the rhythm/atmosphere pairings suggest. For myself, I find that the legato/molding pair suggests the brooding, measured power of a dictator of some kind, while the staccato/floating reminds me of a baby. And staccato/molding equals a robot.

The idea here is to get them to start thinking of these as actor keys or tools to instantly unlock or inhabit character types. We are giving them short cuts that they can use to create characters for subsequent scenework. The only way to stabilize these skills is to try them out. But let's leave that for day three or four.

Object Work

This would be a good day to continue some of the work on imaginary objects and space substance that you started last time. The workshop game 3 Objects starts the group in the direction of performance games and solo work, plus establishing a ground-level assignment that is useful in almost any scene.

To play **3 Objects** the group lines up on one side of the stage and individually enters the performance space, each of them discovering and handling three objects and then exiting the space.

After each one goes through, the audience (i.e. - the remaining players) tries to guess the objects and/or the environment. Evaluation informs the players, again, that we are not looking for them to explain or show the objects being handled. What simply want them to do is to find three objects and exit.

A side point here is the importance of the exit once the task has been completed. There is an improv legend, possibly apocryphal, that Elaine May used to participate in auditions for new Compass Players which consisted of having (male) prospects enter a bar scene in which their objective was to pick her up and get her to go home with them. Elaine's response to any line by the rookie was "Let's go to your place." If the beginner shut up, took her arm and walked out, they passed that test. If they continued the scene without accepting that their objective was achieved, they'd flunk.

It's good to get even beginners aware of this task-based focus, such that they do their job and get offstage, as soon as appropriate.

Having run the entire group through 3 Objects, you can move on, if there's time, to **Add An Object**. In Add An Object someone in the group chooses a location, and the first player comes on stage and "finds" an object, using it appropriately, and then exits. Then the next player enters the same space, uses the same object in the same way, and then finds/uses another object. Then a third player comes in, uses the first two objects and then finds a third, and so on until the entire group has entered and exited.

This game can be very challenging if there are a large number of players. You can also note who has been watching carefully, who will inadvertently skip objects or not give them full reality.

To work on **Time of Day, Occupation and Age** awareness you only need one game: **Bus Stop**. In Bus Stop you have to give stage directions and explanations of what is happening. The players don't generally speak to one another, since they are cast as strangers in the Bus Stop scene.

You ask for four or five volunteers to be in the scene. You explain that they will enter from offstage into the "set." The set is an imaginary park-bench type sitting area (you can use chairs) at a bus stop.

To run the scene as a time of day scene, you secretly assign a time of day to the players and ask them to come into the scene one by one, imagining that it is the assigned time of day. As they one by one enter the set you give information about the status of the bus. First you say that it is two blocks away, then a block away, them a half block, then the bus is pulling up, and stopped. Then you tell them to get on the bus, and when all are on, the scene is finished.

Then you ask the audience what time of day they thought it was. You might try several times in a row with each group, and rotate so that everyone gets onstage. In a discussion after the first one or two tries you should explain that the players are not to try and show or indicate the time of day, but rather to "feel" it and let it affect their bodies as it naturally does each day.

In the age game, first you ask them to secretly choose a number between one and a hundred. Then you tell them that number is going to be their age in the game, and that they must come onstage as a character of that age. Then you tell the audience that their task is to try to guess the age of the players.

You run the same scene as before, with people entering separately. You might want to throw in a curve ball this time by telling them that the bus has broken down or is stuck in traffic a block or so away, and then getting it started again to come to them for the usual pick-up

You then ask the offstage player/audience to guess how old each of the imaginary characters were. Usually they will guess quite accurately. Then you run them through as performers.

Then you can run this same game with occupations, having them select occupations, and having the audience guess what they do. Again, usually the audience will do quite well in selecting the occupations. Again, the concern is to avoid having players telegraph what they do, but rather "occupy" or feel the body/stance/movement/attitude/carriage of their selected occupation.

We want them to gain confidence in the power of that exploration and also in the capability of the audience to figure out who they are. We also want them to understand that it is not important for the audience to figure out the occupation of their character, but rather it is their own exploration that is the focus.

It may be good to explain that this exercise works because both they as players and the audience as observers have had years of study in the fascinating game of people watching, and that they are already quite sophisticated at playing with and interpreting that information.

If time allows, you could play Gemini again, but this time with physicality, or Mr. Know it All and Genre Storyline (see Appendix B).

Summary of Day Two Activities (new items in bold letters):

- Ooga-Booga,
- Inka-Pink,

- Mirror
- Give,
- Give and Take.
- **Three-peat,**
- **Story Circle**
- **Imaginary Rhythms/Atmospheres**
- **3 Objects**
- **Add An Object**
- **Bus Stop:** (Time of Day, Occupation and Age

Game List: (see appendix B)

- Gemini, with physicality
- Mr. Know it All
- Genre storyline

Chapter 6

Workshop #3: The Character in The Scene

On day three we want to give more tools for creating characters, and conclude by looking at scene work. The character work will be based on animal types and the scene work will grow out of that.

We start again with warm-ups, Ooga-Booga, Inka-Pink, maybe Story Circle, and then maybe try another mirror game, e.g. - Verbal Mirror, which is just like Mirror, except you pair off and the follower tries to guess/mirror what the leader is saying. And then switch. This game can be quite funny, and challenging, too. It wouldn't hurt to briefly review the Imaginary Rhythms/Atmospheres circle from Day 2, either.

A workshop game (that can be modified for performance) is **Machine.** In Machine one player enters the stage and starts making a sound and a specific, simple movement. Then another enters and does the same thing. The first player continues with his sound/movement pair. Then a third, fourth, etc. until all players are onstage. To add physicality and create trust you could add the instruction that the players must make physical contact with some other player while doing their movement.

Another layer of challenge would be added by telling them than the contact could not be using their hands. This forces them to find ways of making physical contact that are more inventive and not just an antiseptic hand touch. Again, such physical contact builds trust, familiarity and is far more appealing to a viewing audience.

A variation on this game is **Organic Machine**, in which you ask them to do the same thing but move and verbalize in a more organic plant or animal-like fashion. This completely changes the flavor of the "machine," and can create some fascinating visual and auditory effects. See Appendix B to learn how to turn this into a performance game.

In the previous lesson we had them focus on time of day, age and profession as performance variables. As a warm-up game today you might introduce **Next Room and Last Room**, which require an awareness of location. The way Next Room works is that a solo player enters the performing space, plays a short scene alone, and then exits. The focus of the game is that the player is about to enter the "next" room, which is a particular (imaginary) room or environment of her choice, and that fact influences how she acts in the room in which we see her.

For example, the player may imagine that the next "room" is outer space, and therefore the room we see her in is an airlock where she dons her spacesuit. Or the next room could be the wedding chapel where she is getting married. Or it could be the gas chamber. Any such choice would necessitate physical and postural choices that will fill the scene that we see with believable action.

After the individual players do their scene, the other players try to guess where she was going. It's fun to try to do this, although we don't want the player to "telegraph" in an obvious way where they are going. It clarifies their previous onstage activities for the viewers, and allows for more effective evaluation.

Last Room is the opposite exercise, in that the player arrives onstage having left a room of their choice. Examples might be a prisoner walking out of prison, someone getting off of work, leaving an interview, having broken up with someone, or even a soul leaving the body on its way out of a hospital room.

These games show performers that making choices onstage gives them enough believable activity to comfortably fill out a scene, even with no dialogue. They learn that they can carry a solo scene comfortably, if they have something to do.

The main exercise for the day is **Animals**, which develops characterizations and ends up in scene work. In Animals, you assign individual animal types to each player. Then you run them through a progression.

They start by discovering the animal's body. If it's an animal on all fours, that's where they are. If they are a snake, they are on their belly. The side coaching here is: "Feel the animal's body. How does it move? How fast is it? Is it sneaky, jumpy, smooth?"

Having done that, you ask them to start making the sound of their animal. Then you ask them to get up on their feet, still retaining the basic body, movement and sound characteristics of their animal.

Once they have experimented with that, you ask them to come up to an imaginary party with a buffet table set center stage and interact, but using human voices that retain the character of their animal's sound. You let them continue this scene a bit, during which time you may have to side coach "Give and Take" a bit, and then you conclude the scene.

Having done that, you might briefly ask for experiences, and then run the exercise again, giving each one a new animal.

Having done this twice, you can create connections between this exercise and character development by presenting character types and having them suggest an animal that, to them, would represent that character. You might say "lawyer," and you'll get back animal suggestions such as wolf, packrat, or eagle, all viable suggestions of different types of lawyers. "Football player" might elicit animal suggestions such as bear, gazelle, or elephant, depending on the position of player they had in mind. "Secretary" could be a heron, lioness, or bunny rabbit, depending on the type of secretary that the player envisions.

Having done this, you then have them try to

Paul Johan Stokstad

accelerate the exercise by going through the entire process of animal-body-voice-character almost instantly. To do this you assign them a character type offstage and have them make their own animal decision and enter the same imaginary party and interact, in character, and then exit.

When all are exited, you could assign a new character and do the same thing again, or this time give them an animal and let them come up with the occupation.

What we are hoping to develop is the capability of coming up with believable characters in an instant. By exploring the many physical and postural choices that it takes to express animal qualities onstage, we expand the range of choices that a player feels that they can make. We give them some tools that they can use, if they want, to instantly enter into a character and have a distinct physicality.

They may or may not ever use these tools again. In any case they will have discovered some new possibilities for performing onstage. But if they want, they may continue to use such exercises or choices to instantly add depth to their physical and verbal choices onstage.

At this point you might want to discuss the difference between workshop games and performance games, since you will have to start introducing a lot of performance games if you ever want to create a performing group out of this teeming mass of students. The differences are simple, in that workshop games develop improv skills and ensemble awareness, while performance games are there to display those skills. Of course, the effect of workshop games finds its way onstage in the performance games, and performance games were originally just workshop games. It's just that the people who have started to present the games as a stand-alone entertainment medium have found that certain games have more appeal for a viewing audience.

Freeze and Switch is one of the most famous performance games. This is an ideal game to introduce at this point because it is lively, quick, fun, and it involves all of the following: scene rules, teamwork, give and take, physicality, mirroring, and both physical and verbal justification of some bizarre positions.

To start the game you ask for two volunteers and then get a suggestion for a physical activity for the two. They start a scene with that activity, and after a bit of activity, one of the offstage players will say "freeze" and enter the scene, tapping one of the frozen players out, taking the exact position of the tapped out player, and then justifying that position in a new way by beginning a scene that is unrelated to the previous activity. Then that scene runs for a while until some-one freezes the scene and again taps in and taps someone out, and repeats the new scene process.

Now, that sounds simple, but there are many considerations already in play that need to be brought to the attention of your players.

The first thing is that as players in the

mini-scenes that develop between freezes, they have all of the requirements of scene rules to consider, such as Give and Take, Make Contact, Say Yes, Make Statements, Share Your Voice, Stage Picture, etc. You may have to side coach to remind them of these factors.

The other thing to remember is that the players who are offstage have specific responsibilities. First of all (a personal preference), the offstage players shouldn't be looking for opportunities to freeze the scene so that they can come in with some witty remark that some onstage character's position brings to mind. For example, Onstage character A may be standing, holding up a light bulb to screw in to a socket in an imaginary ceiling, and offstage player B may freeze them because they have a picture of the Statue of Liberty in mind, and they want to come in and say something in that character, such as, "I don't mind being the Statue of Liberty, but I sure wish the birds wouldn't poop on my hand."

Now that is funny (to me, anyway), but that is not the exercise that we are playing here. The other danger is that the player that was in a particular position when you saw the funny opportunity may have moved by the time they hear the freeze call. Then your brilliant joke disappears.

I don't deny that Freeze and Switch can be run this way, and indeed many improv troupes do it this way. It's a fairly clear signal that they are going for as many laughs as possible. Which is one choice of what to do with improv, and not necessarily a totally bad one.

But for our purposes we have a long-range plan, and such clowning doesn't fit into it, at least not now.

We want to caution the offstage players that they have three consecutive foci. First, we want them to watch the scene onstage and see if they can figure out when the scene is "dying." When the scene at play starts to wind down, one of two things can happen. First of all, the scene may just continue its spiral into some kind of boring exchange. This calls for a major rescue, which is in this case a "freeze" call by an offstage player. Secondly, the onstage players may begin some new action or beat, which is, in effect, almost a freeze and switch of their own.

We ask the players to listen carefully and try to intuit whether the players have more juice for some new initiative within the characters that they have selected. In other words, the offstage players have to be attuned to whether the scene is really dying or whether the onstage two are about to break through with some fascinating new material. The twosome may just be getting going, and moments of silence may not mean that they are giving up, but rather that they are about to emerge.

The last thing that you want to be is the boor who froze an interesting couple just because you (apparently) had no sense of how brilliant they were about to be. Then, of course, you are stuck onstage with the onus of doing better.

It's a judgment call, but one which only be made within a group of careful players with an intimate knowledge of each other. That's part of what's called "ensemble," which is a crucial element that must exist in any onstage improv team. It's not just needed, it's the reason why people come to watch, to see good teamwork by people in at least low-grade danger.

So, listening for the scene to start dying is the first focus, which should be followed by an immediate "freeze" call. This freeze is a rescue call for the players onstage. This, too, is part of the ensemble mentality. The beginner may think "I'm not freezing anyone, that means I have to get up there." But the team player thinks, "they need me, I have to save them," and knows that other team players will save them, too. It's a trust thing, and a team player thing.

Getting the shy player out of their worries and into a group mentality is the first step out of their shell and into the protective womb of the group. That protection comes with responsibilities, of course, but then the others are responsible for you, too.

You'll notice how all of these considerations would be ignored by the player who is simply waiting for the two onstage players to get into some funny position that he can freeze and then show off with. Some great scenes can be killed that way. On the other hand, it is a valid way of playing the game, as long as everyone knows when and why.

Focus number two in Freeze and Switch is to be observant and take the exact position and even facial expression of the player that you are tapping out. This calls on the skills that we developed in the mirror games earlier. Finally we ask them to justify the position that they are in some new way. This physical justification gets another scene started with little trouble, and is a delight to a viewing audience.

The magic of that moment is that the player is only asked to justify the position in some new way, not to create a fascinating, comedic scene for two people. The latter may evolve out of the former, but that is not the new player's immediate job. All he has to do is the justification, and then it is the responsibility of the player left over from the other scene to "say yes" by moving into the new situation, while justifying (if necessary) their position, and away we go until the next freeze.

The joy of this exercise at this point is that it demands an integration of everything that has been learned thus far, from both maintaining game focus (giving the player/observers three to sequentially apply) to playing short scenes with scene rules fully in force. It also begins to build a sense of taking care of each other onstage with rescues and freezes. This kind of ensemble activity is the seed for of some of the most sophisticated long-format improv on the planet.

So we plant the seed and start watering it, as of day three.

If time allows, you may want to introduce a

few more performance games here, such as Mr. Know It All (if you haven't already). The current list that we've tried should include Gemini, Genre Storyline and Mr. Know it All. You might catch up on those if you didn't get to them before. If you have already done all of those, you might try Foreign Expert.

Summary of Day Three Activities (new items in bold letters):

- Ooga-Booga,
- Inka-Pink
- Story Circle
- Imaginary Rhythms/Atmospheres
- **Verbal Mirror**
- **Machine**
- **Organic Machine**
- **Next Room**
- **Last Room**
- **Animals**
- **Freeze and Switch**

Game List: (see appendix B)

- Gemini
- Genre Storyline
- Mr. Know it All
- **Foreign Expert**

Chapter 7

Workshop #4: Introduction to Performance

On this day we need to pull everything together that we have been working on and move into more performance games in preparation for getting our rookies ready for actual performance. While it may seem astonishing that we could get a performing group out of players that have only met for four sessions, we can actually do just that.

The reasons for this haste are several. First of all, everyone takes the workshops more seriously if they are actually going to perform in front of a live audience. If they know that they are going to perform they will generally listen to your every word, because they don't want to look bad onstage.

Plus, even though there are many benefits and applications of improv games other than performance, such as team-building in corporate settings, script development for writers, and play rehearsals, improv is all about freeing people up to perform in front of groups.

Many players will lose interest unless there is a potential audience.

These four sessions are actually the basic training for your group that the original players and any players that will be added need to go through. The real growth will happen when this loose association of individuals goes through the rehearsal and performance process, which will typically bind them together like a group of Marines under fire.

After doing our warm-ups, i.e. Ooga-Booga, Inka-Pink, and Story Circle, we could introduce one more workshop game before we plunge into the performance game list, i.e. - **Lemmings.**

These workshop games often affect onstage performances when some scene starts to resemble a workshop game and two players will fall into that workshop game situation as a shorthand means of informing or structuring the scene. An example might be Freeze and Switch, where two recently unfrozen players are facing each other and instantly start playing the mirror game.

Lemmings definitely can influence group scenes, since it involves the entire onstage crowd in a specific activity. In Lemmings, everyone onstage must move together. If someone notes that there is a turtle upstage left, all players go up there to see it. Then someone may say, "Oh, look at the sunset," moving downstage center. Then someone says, "I lost my sunglasses," and moves upstage right, followed by everyone else.

The point is that the group stays together. The subtlety comes into play when, even though the entire group moves together, they may not all have the same motivation. Creating motivation for yourself in the midst of a group movement adds challenge to the game and texture to the scene.

Let's say that in the Lemmings scene described above, when the person says, "I lost my sunglasses," and starts moving upstage right, another person says, "Oh, I think you knocked them off the bench," and another "finds" them and says, "Here they are!" In that case the entire group has moved in the direction indicated by the impetus from the original speaker, but they have not blindly followed, they've each found justification or motivation for that move.

I guess that would be a bunch of smart lemmings or something, which could, indeed, be a new game (new games may come to mind at any time – don't fight it!). In **Smart Lemmings** the group would still move to the same spots, but you might have the players move at different times, each with their own line or motivation. You see how it goes. A game like this could be the hidden agenda in a planned performance scene.

To begin establishing a sense of how scenes work it would be good to introduce a game called **Three Part Scene**, and to discuss it in detail. Playing this game with six players will lay a foundation for having two people do a believable, highly textured scene.

Three Part Scene requires three groups of two players each. Each group has a specific task within the game. The "audience" is asked to select a location and a relationship for the first two players. The first two players go onstage and establish the scene, then they are frozen and switched out by the second two players, who are in turn frozen and switched out by the third set of players, who conclude the scene.

The task of the first group is to enter the scene, in character as suggested by the audience, and handle three objects (each) onstage, thereby establishing a physical reality for the scene. The second group watches closely to see when the first group has accomplished their three objects task, then freezes them and takes their places in the scene.

At this point the second group has the task of discovering and exploring some problem within the scene. The challenge here is not the discovery, but the exploration, since for some reason it is difficult for people not to instantly fix any problem that comes up. If one player discovers a problem and the other immediately fixes it, there will be no way to get the third group onstage since it's their role to resolve the problem that the second has created.

When we say, "explore the problem," we mean explore the implications of the problem. We need the second group to amplify how awful things are with the advent of the problem.

For example, (I'm making this up as I go), the first group may have been given the identity of co-workers in a furnace room, and the first group establishes the location of a furnace and some tools and gauges. The second group may discover that the furnace is starting to overheat, but they can't stop it. That establishes a problem

One of the second group players may start to explore the problem since, for example, heat gives them the hiccups, and then he starts hiccupping. Then the other says he can't stand the sound of hiccups. Then one says, "By the way if the furnace explodes and we get killed there's no insurance coverage, because of the incompetence clause." Then one mentions that he has a pacemaker that will explode if the temperature gets above 150 degrees.

When all this gets to a fever pitch, i.e. – when the third group believes that the second group has discovered and fully explored the problem, the third group can enter, solve the problem, and finish the scene.

By learning this performance game your players will begin to get a sense of how to structure a complete scene, by establishing a physical environment, followed by problem discovery, exploration and resolution. This is a fundamental building block or precursor of almost all stories and mythic tales, which build on individual scenes that explore the growth of individual characters through struggle and resolution.

Such a scene can meaningfully engage and satisfy an audience. This training, if applied properly, can add richness to onstage scene work and in games such as Scene from Nothing, Screenwriter, Rescue, (see appendix B) and the various long-format "Harold" structures (see Chapter 14).

Having worked on all this you will have set the stage, at least, for further growth in skillful scene work, ensemble development and performance capability.

To create a functioning performance group from this raw material you will have to introduce and practice a core set of performance games that everyone knows. A competent group would at least be expected to know the games listed as Groups A and B below, from which you could choose eight or ten games to constitute an improv game-based show (see show structure types, Chapter 9).

I would suggest that Group A would be the first to get started, and Group B could be added as you rehearse for shows and continue with troupe workshops. All of these games and their performance presentation clues are described in detail in Appendix B.

If you can get through all of the new items in Group A in this fourth workshop you will have performed a minor miracle. It's probable that another workshop will be necessary to stabilize both the A and B lists. Once you know who is actually going to perform you will be able to fill in the gaps in ongoing workshops and rehearsals.

Group A

- Gemini (already done in workshop 1 or 2)

- Mr. Know It All (workshop 1 or 2)
- Machine (workshop 3)
- Freeze and Switch (workshop 3)
- Park Bench
- Slideshow
- Foreign Poet
- Foreign Expert
- Genre Storyline

Group B

- Phone Bank
- Dubbing
- Chameleons
- Sportscasters
- Playbook
- Three Part Scene (workshop 4)
- Shrinking and growing
- Screenwriter/SFX

(See appendix B for games on these lists that we haven't covered thus far.)

There are many, many more games, and more are being created daily. Keeping a record of who has experience with what games will be valuable in scheduling rehearsals, shows, competitions, etc. You will need to establish a baseline of game competence so that everyone has a similar toolset. This becomes even more complex and crucial as groups grow and clone off new groups, or compete/play with other groups.

This initial set of four classes establishes a

basic set of agreements that all new players and troupe members can be expected to own. So, you can use these four classes as the training requirements for any incoming players. Such workshops can build up your troupe and/or create complementary troupes.

At this point you will need to get commitments from workshop members that want to become performers. This is when the real fun starts.

Chapter 8

Organizing the troupe

➤ Good prospects

➤ Poor Prospects

➤ Politics/Structure

➤ Volunteers

It's hard for me to predict what form your troupe will take. You may have an established group of kids that you are trying to form into an ensemble for a single show. You may have a group of adults that you are training from whom you are going to pick and choose to create the ideal ensemble. Maybe you are giving a series of workshops, each of which will result in a performing group that will work together as an ensemble for the life of the group.

There are many ways to structure an ensemble and there are many ways to start a group and keep it alive. I'll be discussing group longevity in detail later. But for now I'm just going to assume that you are forming a single performing group out of the four initial workshops that we have just reviewed.

The major challenge is often not one of deciding whom to leave out but rather determining who is truly available. The major qualification that I wanted from my aspirant performers was simply that they would show up for rehearsals, workshops and shows. It's hard to find anyone who isn't busy with something or other, school, work, boyfriends, sports, etc., and you have to know that they are going to make the troupe a priority in their life.

The minimum commitment that they will have to make is a workshop, a rehearsal and a show every time they get onstage with an audience.

They need workshop time because a graduate of four classes is far from complete as an improv performer, since completeness takes practice and there are many new games that they need to know, plus the strength of the group needs to be constantly maintained and deepened.

Rehearsals are necessary, at least at first, since even though they may have played a game once, they may not truly have a sense of how to do it in a performance context. In addition, such rehearsals give a run-through of the entire show so that scene and game changes can be practiced and streamlined.

They have to be able to perform, too, or they don't get the trial-by-fire stabilization of their improv skills that makes it all real. Often people will say that they want to play the games but don't want to perform. This is typically based on an incomplete understanding of how safe playing improv games can be, even with an audience present.

There is a value to playing improv without an audience, which is explored in depth in improv-based executive creativity and team-building programs.

Still, I believe that live performance is the true test of improv, and that you can get people there, despite their fears. You don't need to sell them on this idea before they have taken the classes. But having participated they may see how it can be easy to perform, and even begin to enjoy it.

There is a lot of business to be handled in a performing group; hence you will need to have troupe meetings to sort it all out. The first meeting will be important for laying out the rehearsal schedule, performance schedules, and what their responsibilities will be.

In a volunteer group (and there are very few paid professionals in the improv world) you will be dealing with people with time conflicts and other commitments. This comes back to my first point, which is that attendance is my first criterion for judging potential troupe members. If a troupe member couldn't make the previous workshop and the rehearsal, I would have them sit out the show. They may not like it, but you have to set some boundaries, and establish some motivation for attendance.

Once they get over their fear of performance, they will be clamoring for onstage exposure. I've found that you can't really keep a group of people together unless you either pay them or give them onstage time in front of an audience.

The first troupe meeting sets the stage, therefore, but you'll have to have more as time goes on, to smooth out the wrinkles, the egos, and make agreements in the real world that will support saying yes onstage.

Good Prospects

A good prospect is someone who is open, friendly, curious, plus endowed with intelligence and physicality. We are looking for team players here, not for people who want to be the star. You want people who are willing to try new things with a minimum of fuss about it. You won't always find such people. Oh, and did I mention that you want them to be able to make it to the workshops, rehearsals and shows. It would also be good if they were not above helping out here and there with posters, camera set-up, taking tickets, or whatever.

You are not necessarily looking for extroverts here. Often a soft-spoken type will emerge out of the shadows with some amazing, deft work. Plus you need a variety of player types in order to have a well-rounded experience for both players and audience members.

I like working with married couples. If they both come it brings the entire family in, and scheduling and rehearsal times are less of a challenge.

Bad Prospects

Profile A: The class clown. This guy is used to being the center of attention, and unless he is willing to play along with the group he can be frustrated in improv, because he will not be the sole focus of attention. At the same time, he may be able to learn to relax and let the group carry the ball, and finally be able to relax onstage. He has to learn to trust that others will fill the silence, if he will just shut up. Sometimes, of course, the silence is already full. On the other hand, you will hardly have to discipline this guy, since if he clowns around in improv, the other players will hate him for you.

Profile B: The trained actor. Sometimes these guys are so set in their ways that they can't relax onstage and be themselves. They may not actually have a clear sense of self, because they have been playing so many other people for years. This can result in stilted participation in scenes and games. Acting has lines. Improv has no lines. It's a big leap.

Profile C: The complainer. This person doesn't want to do anything new. It's amazing that such a person would show up, because you would think that a person into improv would realize that they will be doing new stuff all of the time. Still, this person will resist trying new games and wants to stick with what they already know. The fact that they've only known what they know for a week doesn't stop them from preferring that to some new game that you are introducing today.

Profile D: The prima donna. This person wants to perform but doesn't want to set things up, put up a poster, clean up afterwards, or sell cookies at the break. In other words, they want to have the fun but not help make it happen. This is no problem unless that means that you have to do all of those things yourself. Everyone needs to understand that improv is basically a volunteer thing and they are all there to make it happen. Without that you are going to burn out pretty fast.

Profile E: The student. Students in general do not own their time, and can't typically commit to rehearsals and performances. Plus they are a fairly transient population, at least on the collegiate level.

Politics/Structure

There are probably a million ways to structure this, and I certainly have done several of the wrong ones in my day, but you might consider a few such as:

1) The producer/troupe model. - In this model, you are the director and producer. You train people (hopefully for a fee), and then select certain graduates of your workshops to form a troupe. The troupe members enjoy participation based on maintaining a good relationship with you and their co-players, but you are the ultimate authority and decision maker regarding their participation. As the weeks go by you may need to meet with them individually and collectively to discuss things, but you will set policies and they can love it or leave it. This is the typical theatrical director/producer model. It may be a bit challenging to maintain this model if you are also performing in the group.

2). The Player/Coach model. In this model you are more of an equal, and you have meetings occasionally in order to discuss things, but you still make the final decisions. The challenge here is that you often are relying to a large degree on volunteerism on the part of your participants, and so have to keep them interested, you have to entertain them in some ways. To do that, you may need to delegate responsibility as well as work assignments. There is one school of business thinking that says that you should always be training your replacement so that you can keep moving up the corporate ladder. In this model, you will be looking for people who want to learn to train others, run the lights, arrange the publicity, etc., but you will have to give them the authority to make decisions and even money at some point, so, you must be willing to do that before you start down this road.

3) The Co-op model. In this model there is no real leader, just a group consensus. The group may elect a group leader and you may be that person, but your decisions may be countermanded at any time by the wishes/vote of the group. This may be a great model for a free-floating self-contained improv group, but such a structure may not further your particular performance goals.

4) The Venue/Team model. You can set up a performance and training entity and as you train groups they form up teams with any old structure that they want and you simply invite the teams to perform on your stage. You set the rules for performance and they must comply or not participate. You will do well to be open to ideas and creative input from your participating troupes, but you can leave the interpersonal politics to the individual groups.

Volunteers

You'll need help. You can get it, too, from troupe members, their moms, their friends, anybody. The best method is to set up chairpersons to handle each aspect of the show. That includes, at the least:

Poster design
Poster posting
Public service Announcements (PSA's- for radio)
Newspaper publicity - press releases
Tickets and ticket takers, if any
The Money - taken at the show
Bookkeeping
Video taping (don't get me started, more on this later)
Food for the cast
Food/drinks for the audience
Cleaning the theatre
Props, if any
Costumes, if any
Lighting
Music talent coordinator
Music equipment coordinator
Sound Coordinator

The only problem with using volunteer chairpersons for each of these things is that unless they get a back-up support person, the instant that they can't do something (their aunt dies, car breaks down, time of month, hung over, etc.) they will call you and beg off, and that leaves you holding the ball. And then there's another ball, and another, until all of a sudden you are a juggler.

The solution that I came up with for that one is that each chairperson needed a back-up chairperson so that they wouldn't call me when they were blown out of the game. Otherwise your life will become a zoo with no bars and all the zebras, elephants, tigers and pythons will start streaming off into the night streets of downtown Manhattan.

Chapter 9

- ➢ Organizing the show

- ➢ Game Review Format

- ➢ Competition format

- ➢ Improv/Skits/Guests Format

- ➢ Short/Long Format

- ➢ Scheduling the games

- ➢ Assigning the games

- ➢ Publicity, Tickets, Delegation

- ➢ To Tape or Not to Tape.

Organizing the show

When you decide to get your people out on stage in performance, you'll have to design a show to showcase their talents. Predesigning the show gives you something to rehearse. People may imagine that improv isn't rehearsed, and it isn't in that way that a skit is, but the formats of performance and the ground rules should be deeply familiar to the people that you put onstage.

Once you establish the show format and who's doing what, you can run through the show format in rehearsal and make sure that everyone is familiar with the games and roles that they are assigned, and also smooth transitions on and off stage, etc. It may be that Susie has done Foreign Poet once in a workshop situation, but that extra run-through in rehearsal will refresh her memory as to how to do it and allow her to ask any questions that she may have.

Game Review Format

The easiest scheme is simply to serve up a series of performance games. Since games have been the means of learning improv, it's simple just to assign which games will be done by which players and away you go. Even so there are obvious ways that you can vary the presentation for audience interest.

The main things that you want to consider are the number of players and the physicality versus verbal emphasis of the games. If you have four people in one scene, you might do two in the next. If you have a solo or two-person game, next you might try something with the whole group out there.

Games that emphasize verbal quickness, like it's Tuesday, 3-2-1, and Gemini do well when alternated with physical games like Machine and The Movers.

Another consideration is whether the game has a strong scenic element or not. If the game is playful, like Mr. Know It All, but doesn't really result in a realistic scene onstage, like Scene from Nothing, it might be good to vary the presentation between simply entertaining games and scene games.

Some of the workshop games don't really lend

themselves to performance, and are simply designed to build improv skills. Even so, sometimes a small change to one of these games can make it useful onstage. One example of this would be to start the show by having everyone come onstage and begin milling around as in Give and Take, and then someone calls a freeze, walks around speaking in gibberish, and then concludes their action by giving the focus to someone else, at the same   time saying that person's name. This serves to get the troupe onstage and introduce each player to the audience. The intro would conclude when the original mover was introduced.

In general, though, certain games are more oriented toward presentation, and you will want to design your show around those items.

Certain games are born entertainers, and will almost always charm the audience. Prime examples are Mr. Know It All and Park Bench. They do well early on in the show, and interspersed with more experimental material. Your scene games are less likely to be sure hits, and varying their appearance with these more fun games creates a balanced show.

The fact is that we don't simply want to cater to the audience's desire to laugh. We are not simply creating pratfalls and comedy. We are going for a virtuosity of connection, spontaneity and the serendipitous emergence of something surprisingly fresh and brilliant. The funny stuff will emerge from the sure thing games, but the real magic will emerge from the scenework.

Paul Johan Stokstad

It's best to conclude the show or the first half of the show with a big group piece. There are also games that do well with some preparation, such as Dream in the Life. You'll have to take suggestions for those just before the break and then come back with your semi-planned skit first thing after the punch and cookies.

A sample Game Revue Format show would be the following:

Give and Take Entrance (described above)
Gemini (2 performers)
Mr. Know It All (3 performers)
Entrances and Exits (3-5 performers)
Foreign Expert (2 performers)
Hitchhikers (3-4 performers)
Shrinking and Growing (entire cast)

BREAK

Dream in the Life (entire cast)
Park Bench (4 performers)
Dubbing (4 performers)
Sportscasters (2 performers)
Chameleons (2 performers)
The Movers (4 performers)
Scene from Nothing (2 performers)
Screenwriter (entire cast)

For the purposes of analysis, let's look at this show structure and the logic behind it

We start with Give and Take (as described above) to get people onstage and give them something easy to do, and also do a bit of an intro for the crowd. Gemini gives us a sample word game that is charming and fun for the audience, loosening them up a bit. Mr. Know It All brings more people on stage, is a bit more sophisticated and involves the audience directly in an engaging question and answer format. Entrances and Exits creates the first real scene of the evening, but uses a comic device that pushes people off and onstage. It gives more scenic freedom to the players than the structure of the previous games. There's an intrinsic comic element, and the audience is in on the joke because they helped pick the words that push people off and onstage. Foreign Expert is a kind of trick game that involves strong physicality and what appears to be an almost psychic connection between the players. There are only two players, which contrasts with the surrounding games. Hitchhikers is a fascinating ensemble piece, with a preset automobile interior environment. Concluding the first half with Shrinking and Growing, we show the entire cast in a series of short scenes, in an exquisite unfolding and then refolding structure that creates a satisfying conclusion.

BREAK

Dream in the Life gives a personalized, audience-specific visual interpretation of one person's day by the entire group. This features elements from the life of one audience member, which draws the audience in to the show in a sort of conspiratorial revelry. This also demonstrates what the group can do when they have some time to plan things out a bit. This particular game can use slow motion and dance-like effects to good advantage, bringing different flavors of pacing and visual appeal to the show. Park Bench is an almost guaranteed site gag, but static by definition. Dubbing is a scenework challenge, which shows a bit of virtuosity if done well. Sportscasters–a fun concept, verbally interesting. Chameleons–my favorite game, requiring sensitive attunement and physical awareness on the part of the players, and since the viewers provide the beginning and ending scene, it comes to a recognizable conclusion. Movers–another scene challenge. Scene from Nothing–a virtuoso piece, showing that you really don't have to have anything from the audience to do a scene. Once you've established that none of these scenes are rehearsed, the audience can be wowed with this one, if it's explained properly. Screenwriter–involves the whole cast in a complete story that has a beginning, middle and end, sound effects, a narrator, etc.

This of course is just one potential selection of games, but you get the drift.

Improv/Skits/Guests Format

The previous format can be enhanced with other performances to create more of a variety show quality. When you do improv, sometimes you come up with characters that you would like to work with again. The improv scene that birthed the character may be over in a few seconds, but you may want to explore that person and that situation further in a finished comic scene. This is a minor point in my book, but such exploration and the resultant scenes are the entire thrust of troupes such as Second City.

In the early days, no one seemed to have a sense that improv games themselves would be worth watching in a paid venue. Viola Spolin's work seemed to be targeted primarily at creating effective actors using games as a tool, and Second City (and it's hyperextended versions, SCTV and Saturday Night Live) to this day is all about finished comic skits.

Finding players with enough time to train and rehearse in improv plus create new skits each week can be challenging, but it can be done.

I always booked some kind of singer along with each show that we did early on, and would have them sing at the break and at the end of the show. Sometimes it was fine, and other times it was a completely different mood than the show itself.

I used to start the shows with a bit of stand-up intro, and later booked other cast members or visiting comics to kick it off/warm up. If your emcee is a talented comic, it can help. But the emcee plays such crucial role in starting and stopping scenes, that you need to be careful about giving the whole show over to someone who's funny themselves but brain dead about improv.

I've also done shows with a musical parody theme, kind of like the group "Capital Steps" out of D.C. Broadway tunes are easily rewritten with new lyrics, and away you go. We did a "Man of la Muncha" parody with a food theme. It's not hard to think of a parody of "Rent" called "Runt," or a show called "Joseph and the Amazing Technicolor Hard Drive." This type of thing works best as a sort of song medley with or without a loose story tying it all together.

The final product could include half song parody, half improv games, with or without a featured singer/stand-up comic.

In one of my best troupes, we had an 80 year old accompanist who could play any Broadway tune either from memory or with a "Fake Book" of easy arrangements of the same, and he would play as the audience entered, do accompaniment on the songs, and was a general delight to all. Later piano players would even improv along with the scenes as we did them, but more on that later.

The challenges in this format are finding the time to coordinate and rehearse all of the external elements. Every performer has their peculiar needs for a particular mike set up or ego stroking. All that plus running the troupe and performing can get a bit hairy.

We (the cast) also served a snack at the break, ("Snack Theatre, less pretentious than Dinner theatre, and Sweeter") which was endearing to the audience, and also a quick way to find out who were the real prima donnas in the cast.

Competition format

It may be that the majority of improv troupes in the world perform in a competition format. The champs of this style are the Theatre Sports and Comedy Sports franchises that are active in the U.S., Canada, Australia, and Japan, and I suppose many other countries (by now).

Keith Johnstone was struck by the audience involvement evident in sporting events and probably with a desire to deflate the formality that can haunt presentations of traditional theater, decided to stage improv shows in a competition format, with two teams vying for points.

Typically each team of 2 to 6 players will perform the same improv challenge and there will be a score awarded to each team, with the highest scoring team overall winning the night. The Theatre Sports format features a set of judges chosen from the audience (or pre-arranged celebrity judges from the community) who evaluate the success of game and scene challenges based on pre-established criteria such as narrative or storytelling excellence, technical accomplishment, entertainment value, etc.

The audience is often encouraged to throw popcorn or even foam bricks (called boo-bricks) at the judges if they disagree with the scoring. This format can be dramatized in many ways, such as using an emcee with a whistle and a referee's shirt, a buzzer at the half, a scoreboard, etc.

A visit to a competition based improv show will give you the idea. It's also possible that this could be a section of a larger show, serving as one half or even just one game challenge within one of the formats described above.

Short/Long Format

There is another, equally fanatical group of performers who do nothing but long-format improv. Most, but not all of them live in Chicago. Since I have an entire chapter on long format later I don't want to go into much detail here, but at least wanted to mention that balancing the long-format stuff with a series of games could make for an interesting show. I would suggest that games in the first half followed by a long-format set in the second half would make for a challenging and compelling evening.

Assigning the Games

It's best if you create a kind of grid with the game names down the left column and the game assignments on the right. That way you can see who you've put when and effectively share the load (and the limelight), plus provide a variety of faces for the audience to enjoy.

You'll find that performers are very alert to being shorted in stage time, which is not surprising, since they've worked so hard and this is a kind of a payoff as well as a trial by fire for them. In addition, if someone has just been doing something strenuous, you can rest him or her in the next scene.

This list also serves as a show template for the emcee, the musician, the performers (backstage) and the program (if any).

Publicity, Tickets, Delegation

I'm assuming that you know that you will need posters, ads, public service announcements (radio, maybe TV), etc. Every town is different. In some places little photocopied posters on day-glo papers will get you the crowd you are looking for. In other towns it's the shopper, the free art/events magazine, or the radio plug. In any case you have to investigate where people find out what's happening (if you don't already know) and get your stuff visible in that place.

Tickets may or may not be necessary. It all depends on whether you have advanced sales or not. If so, you may get by with a trainee taking tickets, or someone who says they can't afford the classes or the show.

The challenge of all this is that you have already trained the troupe, scheduled the gig(s), and designed the show, and you still have to choose what you personally are going to wear (something you don't mind wearing while you are crawling on the floor).

You need to learn to delegate or you will burn out with your first show. I once worked with a novice director of a regular dramatic production and she went into gridlock two weeks before the opening and couldn't answer the simplest question. You don't want it to be that way. Your burnout is perhaps the main obstacle to the longevity of the troupe.

The only sensible solution is that you have as your long-term goal a situation in which you do nothing for the show but show up. You should delegate everything that you can. And then delegate the delegation. One principle of business success that I've heard is that you should always be training your successor. If you don't do that, you can never move up the ladder and leave the unit that you were working in intact.

If you are always over worked, you won't retain the overview that's necessary to maintain and grow a complex project of this sort.

The additional policy that you will need (as I stated earlier) is a second layer of delegation. That is, no one that you delegate to is allowed to get back to you if they drop the ball and leave it in your hands. If the postering person gets sick, they have to have a previously arranged back-up that's not you. It doesn't take very many balls dropped back in your lap before you are going to be crazier than a cat juggler in a mouse colony.

You need to take care of yourself. But more on that later.

Paul Johan Stokstad

To Tape or Not to Tape.

The answer is yes and no. Yes if you are not in the show and don't have anything else to do that night. Yes if you have someone else that knows what they are doing AND what you are doing. Otherwise, no.

It turns out that videotaping a show effectively is just as difficult as putting on the show itself. It takes hours of preparation laying down cords, mikes, plus possible time spent editing the tape. You may need three or more people to do it right. You probably don't have three or four extra people or any money to pay them.

On the other hand, a simple tape of the show can be quite valuable for review later. Even so, there is still the set up time, lugging cameras about, etc. Plus anyone who is taping the show can't really enjoy the show fully. It takes a special person who is willing to do all that.

Hopefully you will find one.

My dream set up includes a live three-camera shoot run by one person with remote auto cameras that he controls, with maybe a hand-held thrown in just for fun. So far no lottery win, so I don't have the 200k worth of equipment just yet.

But if you do, let's talk.

Chapter 10

Show rehearsal

- ➢ Introducing the show structure
- ➢ Assignments/Negotiations
- ➢ Adjustments

Introducing the show structure

Once you have it all set up, you have to explain it to the players in the show rehearsal. Having a rehearsal of each game, by the players assigned to each, in the order specified by the show plan, is a good idea for a number of reasons.

First of all, such rehearsal reminds the players of how to play each game. It may have been a few weeks or even months since this particular player played that particular game. Typically the player has never performed that assigned game in front of an audience. If they have, it's more likely that you would give someone else a chance on that game. So, almost every time each game assignment is a bit new or rusty for the assigned player.

Running through the game reminds them of the game rules, plus the particular foci of the game, and the little performance tricks that make raw improv games more palatable/presentable to an audience. It may be that your group has never performed that game live, and the performance elements will have to be worked out on the spot. I'll be giving you performance tips on many games in Appendix B, but you may find that you have or want to come up with refinements of your own.

Rehearsal also smoothes the transitions between games, including any props or game set-ups, plus at least initially imprinting in the players heads when they have to be onstage, and who else has to be there with them.

I usually give out a copy of the game list and the assignments to each player. They inevitably lose it by the time we perform, so I keep and post a copy on the backstage wall on show night. Even so, if they have the overview in their hands in rehearsal, it's a help.

Assignments/Negotiations

People will sometimes want to be re-assigned or to switch roles with someone else. If you can make these changes without significantly compromising the principles that gave you the original structure, great. Often the performers will simply have performance anxiety and will be imagining difficulties at every turn. You'll have to encourage them that it will all work out, which it usually does, since our expectations of "success" in improv performance are set pretty low in comparison to, for example, traditional theatre.

Sometimes the game will seem like a disaster in rehearsal, and everyone's disaster antenna will go up. Other times it will be phenomenal in rehearsal and lack that greatness in performance. The reverse logic sometimes evolves that a "bad" rehearsal generally means a good show, while a good rehearsal could result in a flat performance. It does seem to go that way a lot of the time, though there is no apparent conclusive reason for such a phenomenon. In any case, it's good to point this out to people, so that they don't get attached to success in either performance or rehearsal.

Of course, people easily forget what "success" in improv means. Regardless of how many times you tell them, they still tend to think of improv in terms of the audience reaction.

But, as we have explained, we are not doing improv for the audience, any more than we play a basketball game strictly for the crowd. In a basketball game, there is a long list of priorities that the player is concerned with more than crowd satisfaction, including executing fundamentals, getting shots in, moving the ball around, running plays, defending, deception, surprise, speed, stamina, competition, as well as determination and will power.

Successful improv would have the following qualities, in descending order of importance:

1. Free-flowing creativity
2. Having fun
3. A strong, intuitive connection with your fellow players
4. Playing by the scene rules that govern all improv games
5. Playing within the challenges posed by each game
6. Presenting the material in a manner that makes it accessible to a crowd
7. Audience enjoyment
8. Audience reaction

Adjustments

The rehearsal may unearth problems in presentation surrounding a particular game. It's typical that the performers will blame the game itself, especially if it's a new one. You may need to adjust the game in some way to make it more presentable, but more typically it was just a matter of the participants in the game not playing it properly, or that they have inflated expectations of the results of the game. Not all games are going to be hilariously funny, at least not every time. And your star performers on most nights will shine less brightly on other nights. That's the value of having a troupe. You never know who will be hot on which night. And it doesn't really matter. There will be great moments and times of less brilliance. The audience is generally amazed and amused that you are even trying.

If you generally have an unforgiving audience, get another gig.

Chapter 11

Showtime

- ➢ Warm-ups

- ➢ Role of the M.C.

- ➢ Neutral Observer

- ➢ Guest Talent

- ➢ Post Ludem analysis

Warm-ups

Your performers are walking in off the street and have their day jobs, relationships, dinner, bills, plus a little trepidation to put behind them. You need to get them into the mindset of a improv performer, a participant in a group event. It's one thing to be a good soldier on the parade ground when you look good and the girls are watching and the band is playing, but to keep order in the ranks when you are marching the same crowd into the jungle, people are shooting at you, you haven't eaten in two days and there's a hole in your foot isn't so easy.

That's why we work together, play together, and get to know and trust each other so deeply before we go onstage, so that those habits are stronger than the concerns about the audience that all of a sudden is in the room as well.

To warm-up we engage in familiar workshop warm-ups like Ooga Booga, Inka Pink, and Story Circle. I also like to remind people of their commitment to each other, sometimes I may have them all say something to each other, like "I will be there for you, I will be there for you, I will be there for you," until they have spoken that out to every other member in the troupe. It may sound hokey, but having stated that, most people will then go out and do it.

Paul Johan Stokstad

I also throw in some group breathing exercises and some of what is called Edu-K, or Educational Kinesiology, which is featured on the website braingym.org. The breath work is to further that sense of unity within the group, which is, after all, what the audience is really here to see: people working together. The Edu-k pulls the player together, centering them in themselves and in the moment so that they have all of their capabilities to bring to bear on the performance task.

The breath exercise is simply to breathe together, which would be hard to do without a physical cue. What we generally do is hold hands in the middle of the group (all the hands in a clump), and raise the hands as we inhale and lower as we exhale. This creates a sense of unity in the group. You need that.

Another thing we do to just kind of kick out the nervousness is to hold hands together just as described above and have them start low between us as we start out with a barely audible group sound which we increase as we slowly raise the hands in the middle and build and build in volume until we end with a shout as we throw our hands in the air. It's exhilarating and crazy, and gets people into a pumped up, go for it mood. They'll need that, too.

There are many Edu-K exercises. They are based on a theory that moving the body in particular ways can stimulate the brain. Usually the brain dictates the movement of the body, but, according to E-K, the tail can wag the dog, in some way, too. To see how this makes sense, let's say that it takes both hemispheres of the brain to move both sides of the body in unison. If we moved both sides of the body in unison, according to the Edu-K view, we might be retroactively stimulating the brain to use both hemispheres. This is possibly the most simplistic explanation of Edu-K ever, but you get the point.

I have borrowed just a few of these, but they are purported to do things like reduce stage fright, "center" the individual in a state of calm, pull the creative and intellectual capabilities into synch (left/right brain), and stimulate listening and speaking skills. All of those things are great for anyone going onstage with no lines and only a game between themselves and a blank stare into the klieg lights.

Here they are (this is just a sample selection of these tools, but these are what I use):

Cross Crawls: For left/right integration. You stand relaxed with your arms at your side. Then you swing your right arm to the left, crossing the mid line of the torso, while you raise your left knee to the right, also crossing the mid line. As you draw the leg and the arm back to where they started, you initiate the opposite leg and arm to do the mirror image of the first set of motions. I.e. - swing your left arm to the right and your right leg to the left. You keep doing this for a period of fifteen seconds or so, then rest. As you move, you inhale and exhale once per complete cycle, relaxing your jaw as you exhale.

Figure Eights: Left/right integration. You stand relaxed, and raise both arms extended in front of you, joining the hands in the middle with the palms flat against each other. Then, pointing with the two hands, you begin to "draw" a sort of sideways figure eight in the air, by lifting your joined hands up and to the left, then circling down and back up through the middle in front of you, then down on the right and back up through the middle. As you raise the hands through the middle you inhale, and on the outside, downward circle you exhale.

Lunges: For stage fright. To do this, you imagine that you have a sword in one hand and you lunge out into a deep stance where your front knee is bent and your back knee is straight out to the side. This stretches the psoas muscle in the leg and pelvic region and is supposed to be a very calming stretch to counteract the jitters.

Ear Rub: For listening. Believe it or not, a firm rubbing of the ears, exploring their many folds in the fingers of your hand is said to stimulate listening skills.

Cook's Hookup: For centered, integrated calm. This is best when done lying down, but it can be done standing, in a pinch (which is where you usually are back stage). It's a bit challenging to describe, but hang in. You stand (or lie) with your right foot placed in front of your left (overlapping). Put your palms together as if you were praying. Then slide your palms around each other so that they are facing the opposite way from the way they normally would face. In other words, your right palm will be facing to the right of your body and the left to the left. You then interlace your fingers. You're almost there. Then you take those awkwardly contorted hands and turn them up inside, toward your chest and rest them on your chest, with the interlaced fingers pointing up toward your head. In this position you simply rest for a few moments. Usually a sort of secure calm will begin to dawn.

These things may seem crazy, but they work. And anything that gets the performer out of their day into the performance space, centered in themselves and focused on the present moment is worth trying.

One more thing borrowed from the Edu-K guys is an emphasis on water. They constantly provide learners with water, and anyone who has experienced pre-show nervousness would probably concur that water is pretty important. Somehow drinking water has a calming, reassuring effect. No one should be left without an abundance of water to drink before and during the show.

Role of the M.C.

The emcee needs to be someone who knows what is happening. In a beginning to intermediate level troupe, the emcee will play a ringleader role, guiding the players, starting and stopping the games, and interpreting the show for the audience.

This is no place for an introvert. You have to feel comfortable getting out there onstage and welcoming the crowd, who after all are already in a good mood because they are here to laugh and be entertained and all they are hoping is that you will not disappoint them. Remember that they WANT you to succeed, since that's what they paid for, so they really are on your side.

You need to give some orientation for new people and explain that the show is completely improvised, and that you will need their help in the selection of locations, character relationships, etc. You may need to explain the challenge of each game as it comes along in order that the audience can be in on the difficulties imposed on the players. The players may add more layers of difficulty on themselves (such as obeying scene rules, picking an animal or rhythm to embody onstage, etc.) but its fun for an audience to be in on the game. There are even some games such as Expert Endowment where the audience knows more than some of the performers, which is usually a source of great audience delight.

You don't need to go into great detail here, just a general orientation. One thing that you could do is practice taking suggestions. You might, for example explain that when you ask for a place suggestion you are looking for a place that will fit on the stage. If for example, someone suggests "France" as a place you might need to ask them to clarify as to where in France did they mean. If they say "Paris," you will continue to drill them until you have the specifics of, say, an outdoor café as your setting.

You could explain that when you ask for a relationship you are looking for a work or blood relationship, where work means boss, employee, co-workers, and blood means husband, wife, sisters, brothers, sons daughters, etc. If they suggest lovers or boyfriend/girlfriend, husband/wife as a relationship, I always have the joke ready that that's a work relationship.

That's all that you want from them, in general, although there are games that involve audience members to suggest words, themes, changes, song genres, or even appear onstage. But we'll get to that.

Over all the emcee is the presenter of the improv material and draws the audience into the show by asking for suggestions. The suggestion element really has as it's primary value a clear demonstration to the audience that what is being presented is improvised, on the spot, for the first time ever. In some sense this is completely a fraud, since the games and the structure and the roles and the deep agreements between the players is totally and completely rehearsed and practiced.

But it is improvised just as a basketball game is improvised. No one really knows what is happening in advance, in terms of the subjects that will be discussed and dramatized. But the likelihood of something fun and enjoyable to watch is high.

The emcee introduces each game, explaining it as needed to the audience, and calls the players onstage. Then he gets the necessary suggestions from the crowd. For most games the emcee will then retreat from the stage for the duration of the game. But they stay alert to what's happening onstage, because when the game has run its course the emcee often needs to step in to conclude the game.

Sometimes this can be done with a blackout, if such lighting control exists in your performance venue. That means that you as the emcee will stop the scene when an appropriate moment has been reached by either cutting the lights yourself or signaling the lighting guy.

This type of decision requires a clear understanding of the goals of the game, how the scene/game is going, and a sense of timing. Often you are hoping for even a semblance of a conclusion or a good laugh so you can get your players offstage.

This is a form of what is called "editing."

Every game has a task and a sort of life cycle of it's own. Remember that when we accomplish our tasks in improv, we find an exit and get offstage. Your performers may sometimes end the game themselves, if they think that it's done. But more likely you, as the emcee, will have to step in. It's delicate, because you don't want to step in too early and stop something brilliant from happening. Sometimes the best stuff comes out just as things apparently have nowhere to go. You just have to get a sense of it.

Ultimately your players will themselves become their own editors, and create ends, transitions and new games all on their own. But more on that later.

Sometimes an improv game will not work very well, and you can rescue the situation with a joke about it, like, "Well, we won't be doing that again..." or some such thing. The point is that you realize and they realize that's it's not all going to be great, but you are out there going for it, and at least it's completely new! Your remarks of amazement (good or bad) on the previous game will sometimes release more laughter, which as you must know, always loves and needs release.

So, play with the crowd, make comments on their suggestions, and drop in a quip or two here and there. Then, at the end, get all your players back onstage, thank the audience for coming, and bask in the glory (if any), as needed.

Paul Johan Stokstad

Neutral Observer

It's great if you have one player (or a director who is not also the emcee, if your players have evolved to the point that they can emcee) who can just watch the show. Maybe all you will have is a video camera, but you need something or someone to record the show and or their reactions to the show in a technical sense. What we are looking for is where improv principles were and weren't being followed effectively, ways that individual games might have been better presented, or technical elements such as lighting or staging that could have been improved. You may not have the luxury of a non-emcee director or one player that will actually sit out a whole show, but you need something.

If you videotape the show, someone (probably you) will have to review it all later. But it's important to do so, because you all want to learn from your front line experience in order to do better next time. A traditional theatrical performance will always conclude, after the show (or before the next performance) with a meeting to give out "notes" for improvement to each person, as necessary. To do this in improv, you might bring along the video as a learning tool. But only if it's easy. Otherwise, you can spend a lot of your time lugging VCR's around or engaging in extra meetings when you need to get into rehearsal.

Guest Talent

Sometimes you'll bring in a guest either as the emcee (as in Saturday Night Live) or to do other acts such as sing or be in some skit. If they are going to be the emcee, they either need to be seriously coached about what to do, or their activities need to be reduced, basically, to introductions. Your players may be able to stop/edit the scenes themselves, or you, sitting by the light button, can conclude matter(s) as they go along.

If you have brought in some singing talent to perform at the opening, intermission and/or end of the show, they will need to be included in the final acknowledgements. You may be able to (if you want) include them in some simple game such as Audience Member (where they are given three lines on a card that they can say at any time).

Just remember that outside talent is typically a challenge, because they all have their particular technical and egoic needs, and somebody will have to see to all that. If you have a dedicated talent person, great, if not, there's one more ball for you to juggle along with the lighting, tickets, directing, training, scheduling, ad sales, printing, and maybe even performing balls that you already have in the air. That's eight balls already, and I think the record for nine is a matter of a few minutes.

Paul Johan Stokstad

Post Ludem Analysis

After the show you are going to need to sit down and make sense of any notes you made during the show, review the tape, and come up with a recipe for what worked and what didn't for the next time. Every jet engine needs maintenance and tweaking after it's high tech lurch into the skies. And improv theatre is no jet, it's a rocket ship that will either shoot around the moon or blow up just after launch on national TV with everyone watching. No pressure, of course.

Chapter 12

Ongoing workshops and Rehearsals

Once you've performed and decided that you need to improve, you'll have to get together and do it.

An ongoing troupe has five major projects running at the same time:

1. Processing what happened last time and learning from it
2. Keeping existing skills and games sharp
3. Learning new skills and games
4. Integrating new people into the mix
5. People issues

We'll talk about points 4 and 5 in Chapter 16, "Keeping it together," but the others we can discuss here.

Reviewing the previous show will either bring up issues of improv principles, individual game performance or game staging. Either you need to review improv basics, the rules and goals of a particular game, or just how that game was presented, introduced or staged will need discussion. Typically someone just forgot some basic improv tenet such as "Say Yes" or

"Stage Picture," etc. Maybe the game wasn't clearly understood. Maybe you, as the director/teacher, didn't explain it clearly enough. Or maybe the game will need some adjustments in order to be amenable to public performance.

In any case, you should do that in your next workshop or rehearsal. The workshop is the place to review and fix broken understandings on your last show, and to introduce new improv principles and games. There is no way that four introductory workshops are going to give your people the seasoning and the knowledge base that they need to be complete performers.

We want them to get out there onstage in order to get a sense that the games work and to have some fun playing them in front of a crowd. And it's a great motivator for them to realize how they blew it and not want to repeat that experience. Believe me, the fact that they know that they are going onstage the first time has a sobering effect on the crowd and can have them hanging on your words more than a simple improv playtime session can do. Knowing that they are going back onstage is even more of an enhancement to their attention span.

You should also have a list of fifty to a hundred improv games that none of them have tried. I'll be giving you a bunch later in this book. You can get more from Bay Area Theatre Sports, Viola Spolin's books, or from any number of other improv books, or by searching under the phrase "improv game" on the web. You may come up with your own new game ideas or game refinements on existing games based on what happened to your people onstage or in rehearsal. Plus, some players who didn't get to do a particular game in a particular show may want to try it next time.

If you have the luxury of having a workshop, a rehearsal and a show every week, you have a highly dedicated group on your hands. You may be able to collapse the workshop and the rehearsal into one session, but, as with anything, you, the performers, and the audience get out of it what's put in into it. Practice makes parfait.

Don't forget to praise them for what went well. As a matter of fact, make sure that you say this stuff first. This will expand the good feeling in the group and then make the points of correction or potential growth easier to swallow. Of course that's Teaching 101, i.e. - Mary Poppins' spoonful of sugar to help the medicine go down. But it's still important, unless, of course they're diabetic, in which case a pat on the back will have to do.

Chapter 13

Musical Improv

Musical improv probably inspires more pre-performance fear and more admiration (and audience approval) than any other type of improv. I believe this is due to the fact that music is deeply connected to the emotions, and it's hard for performers to believe that they could be so vulnerable onstage as to sing without any preparation, and audiences find it impossible to believe that anyone would try.

One thing to remember is that improvised songs, in general, have dopey lyrics and are only sometimes reasonably in tune. But that hardly matters to an audience, since they are so amazed that you are even trying it that they will go wild with admiration and applause if you even get close to something resembling a song.

But it's surprisingly easier than anyone would expect.

When we perform musical improv we generally put up a poster on the wall of a number of musical genres. These correspond to the actual genres that we have practiced singing in rehearsal and are willing to try to recreate onstage. The basic musical improv game is called Song Challenge. In this game, the players are given a location and a relationship, and start a normal scene. As the scene progresses, audience members are allowed to call out "song" at moments in the scene that seem to call for a song.

At that point the audience member who stopped the action gets to choose a musical genre from the list on the wall, and the players onstage must sing a song in that genre, using what's happening in the scene as subject material for the song.

In order to get your troupe to the point where they can do this without first fainting on the spot, you have to spend some time in rehearsal with an exceptional breed of musician, usually a pianist with the ability to play a lot of musical styles and listen carefully to some bad singers and try to adjust to their faltering attempts at a song.

This is the one challenge facing you. Get a good musician and you have a chance to do this well. No good musician, no chance.

Once you have found your brave and talented pianist, you need to bring the virtuoso in to work with your troupe. The pianist may suggest a number of genres that he/she can do, and then your players will get to sing along.

Of course, there's a bit more detail to making this work. First of all, most musical styles (other than opera) generally have a verse plus chorus format. This makes your life a bit easier. In order to improvise a song, all your players have to do is sing one verse and then relax into the chorus. Then another player can sing the next verse.

You might ask, "How do I decide what notes to sing? This is far simpler than it appears to the casual observer. First of all, in musical improv, we usually emphasize genres that you have heard many times over, for many years. If we improvise a pop musical song in the U.S., we will be far more likely to have success than if we tried to do the same thing in the style of Chinese Opera. This is because there is a high degree of experience and shared history among the players with pop music. Most people in the West have heard a lot of pop music and so have a sense of how it goes.

In addition, the music itself subtly guides you toward using certain notes. For example, in a musical scale there are typically certain notes that are dominant, especially (in pop music), the first, fourth and fifth notes (e.g. - in the tune "Louie, Louie"). If you want to finish a song, for example, you tend to arrive back at the base note (the first) in order for listeners to experience a sense of completion.

So, your note choice is somehow subtly guided, and it doesn't matter that much what notes you pick anyway, since the piano will carry the song forward, and then all you have to do is come up with some words. But let's not do that the first time. Let's just sing some notes. That's right, when you are learning to sing musical improv, the best thing to do is to start by making nonsense syllables or gibberish along with singing an improvised tune (along with the piano accompaniment) until you feel confident that you can create music with no words in it. So just get your pianist to play some musical genre and you (and your individual troupe members) can just practice singing nonsense syllables along with it.

Once they have a sense that creating notes is easy, then you can move over to actual words. When the words come in, you are generally looking for a phrase or two, usually with an end rhyme. It wouldn't hurt to practice this skill alone, with no music, that is, have them practice saying a sentence and then another that rhymes with it. This isn't far from what rap musicians do, but first you are going to try it with no music.

One more possible step is to try to do the words with the music, but not singing, just speaking them out, trying to practice your phrasing so that the sentence you speak out not only gets rhymed by the next one, but starts and stops with the musical phrase given by the pianist. That will kind of sound like a rap thing, which is fine.

Finally we put it all together and try to sing along with the pianist.

Having had everyone work on singing one musical phrase each, you can then move on to a more finished piece, and that involves adding in the chorus. The chorus is your friend onstage, in that it gives everyone a rest between singers so that one player can step out of the limelight and another can prepare to jump in.

There are several ways to come up with the chorus. In one version, the first singer has the additional task of coming up with the first chorus. Then, if the choral music is repeated twice by the musician, your players can all jump in and sing it on the first go around. That way they support the first singer and give that player a rest from being on the spot, plus they stabilize their memory of the chorus, because they are all going to be singing it again in 15-30 seconds. In any case, once you have a verse and a chorus, you only need another verse or two and you are done with an entire song. Even the musical champs on "Whose Line Is It Anyway" generally only sing two verses and two iterations of the chorus.

The other way to come up with the chorus involves having one of the other players jump in once the first singer has finished the first verse. This can be the preferred method in some groups, because it takes some of the pressure off of the first singer

Now, I know that this "instant chorus" may sound like an impossible dream, but, oddly, even the musically undereducated can generally determine when a song switches from the verse to the chorus. You might make this a musical workshop game, i.e.- have the musician play several verses and then the chorus, and have people yell out "chorus" when they hear the change.

One thing that will amaze you is how much the rhythm and the music of each genre carries you through this whole endeavor. It's actually harder to sing out of tune than in tune. And the fact is that the music accompaniment will almost always sound good, even if your singing and words are pretty dorky.

Again, the audience will not care, since they fully expect you to fall flat on your face, and if you do anything even slightly resembling a song they will usually cheer your efforts with gusto. If you blow it, they will sometimes cheer just as hard. People can be very forgiving when you are doing something that is apparently this impossible. But it's not impossible, and if you break it down into pieces as I've described, and then put it all together, you very well may come up with something memorable.

And did I mention that a good musician is important?

The fact is that the best musician for you is someone who also understands what you are doing in improv, who has maybe (even) taken your introductory workshops. That musician can even improvise along with every scene that you do throughout your entire show. There are also games such as By the Music, in which the musician determines the tempo and mood of the scene with distinct, dramatic changes in the music.

Many troupes have a musician and a sound specialist, and either one or both may add elements to the show, sometimes from a whole library of pre-recorded sound effects, such as ringing phones, thunder, cat meows, etc. Many digital pianos have a large set of sound effect possibilities that the skilled player can add in to the mix as well.

That takes a committed co-performer. Best of luck on finding that person. If you do, try to keep them happy, since they are worth their weight in attendance tickets.

Overview of a successful song improv:

Scene gives content and character elements
Audience or emcee freezes scene in crucial spot
Audience chooses song genre from list on wall
Pianist plays theme
Players listen and get a feel for song
One player steps out and sings verse
Other players form a curved back line behind main scene singers
Back line starts simple movement appropriate to genre, keying off of player on the end of the row (e.g. - on the right)
Some new player sings one verse of the chorus
All repeat chorus to stabilize it in memory
Next player sings verse
All sing chorus
Next player sings verse
All sing chorus
Repeat chorus with dramatic gesturing and crescendo to finish

Chapter 14

Long Format

Long format improv is one of the most fascinating branches of the improv tree.The growth of this version, at least in Chicago, has been discussed in detail in Kozlowski's *The Art of Chicago Improv*. To summarize that tale, improv participants have long experimented with various formats in which improv could be used to create full-length shows.

Second City in Chicago has full-length shows, but they hardly ever feature improv itself, since they normally use improvisation in rehearsal to generate skit material that finds its way into finished skits and revues. They do have an "improvised" portion at the end of each show, but it is not improvised on the spot, but rather staged after as much as thirty minutes of planning.

Other Chicago groups such as Improv Olympic have developed forms of extended, fully improvised show structures that allow for the creation of 30 to 45 minutes of completely new material based on a single suggestion from an audience. There are many other troupes working on various versions of long format, especially, but not solely, in Chicago.

It's not hard to understand the motivations for this growth. Improv players naturally want to stage shows that are more than simple collections of games. Plus, once you have established that you can be onstage and get laughs easily through improv, you start to wonder if you could do richer more meaningful drama as well.

It doesn't take long for people who have found their dramatic home in improv to dream of doing more serious work with it. Serious means deeper, more exemplary of the totality of human experience. Not everything can be conveyed through the comic. It's satisfying to performers and audiences alike if they can create and/or see an improv show that entertains with wisdom, honesty and insight in addition to humor.

Sometimes, of course, the audience has to be retrained, since improv has been associated with comedy. Improv is often quite funny; if only because of the sense of surprise and childlike joy the audience has in witnessing onstage players magically extract themselves from difficulty after difficulty. Even so, even a comic performance can have also moments of beauty, especially in one of the long format modes.

The most famous long format is called the Harold. It's a made up, non-sense name with no connection to the format itself, kind of like naming your first winter cold "Fred." Even so, the definition of how to do it can be fairly clear. I think a better name would be something like Game Raga or Lotus, since there is an unfolding, cyclical nature to the game.

The Harold form that I will be presenting is a basic version. Long-format troupes that work together six to eight hours a week will obviously evolve this form to the point where it hardly resembles the structure that you'll see below. My Harold form is appropriate for advanced beginners, in that it takes some advanced improv skills, and is challenging, but when your troupe members are far down the road, they may evolve the form into something that is quite a bit more organic and free form. In chapter 16 I will suggest some directions that this might take in my dream team troupe. For anything more, you may have to move to Chicago.

The Harold (version 1.0) begins with a number of activities and games that are designed to stimulate the performers thinking and give them material for creating three distinct scenes. To do that the emcee gets a word from the audience, warning them that this word choice will be the theme of the show for the next 30 minutes or so.

Having selected a word, such as love, money, relationships, departures, discoveries, or even bananas, the troupe embarks on a long journey by spending some time talking about and considering that word. One format is to have the players mill around as they free associate words that the original word brings to mind. Alternately they can stand in a semi-circle facing the audience and do the same thing.

For example, if the theme word chosen by the audience was "puberty," the players might start saying individual words, like pimples, embarrassed, sweating, nervous, changes, funny voice, girls, boys, junior high, wet dreams, or whatever comes into their mind about that topic. This "word patterning" sets the stage for the topic in the minds of players and audience alike.

Then an individual player will break out into some kind of monologue on the topic of puberty. These monologues will usually be some autobiographical story about their experiences from puberty, but may also include opinions, stories that they've heard of relevance, even scientific observations or poetry and song lyrics that reflect light on the topic. Then several other players one by one step out and give their stories/anecdotes/opinions, etc.

Then one player grabs another and starts a scene based on some aspect of the material that has just been presented. If, for example, someone described the agonies that he went through in trying to get up the nerve to kiss a girl, someone may set out to dramatize that scene with another player. That scene runs for a while, until it is edited or interrupted by another scene initiated by another player on some other theme that the initial monologues have inspired. This second scene is itself cut off or edited by a third scene with a third theme or situation.

So, you have done three scenes based on the original suggestion, and you have only started the Harold, because there's a lot more yet to come. Once your three scenes have been established, the troupe chimes in with any number of improv games, songs and even other monologues to add to the richness of the consideration of the topic.

For example, you may have just done three scenes about puberty, but the next thing that will happen is that someone will set up a Mr. Know It All game to answer audience questions about puberty, or bring in a Foreign Expert to talk about it, or show a Slide Show from his junior high school years.

Then the plot thickens, because the players who did the first scene about puberty take the stage as the same characters that they were the first time. The only difference is that they project themselves back in time to a point before the first scene. In other words, if the first scene was about a boy trying to get up his nerve to kiss a girl on a date, the next time we see these two could be a flashback to the moment where he asked her out.

Then, of course, the second scene comes onstage and recreates their characters, also at a point in time before the initial happenings in their first outing, and likewise with the third of the original three scenes.

At this point, all three scenes have run twice, and we are still running down the Harold road at full tilt, because in pops the rest of the troupe members with more games, songs and monologues, all on the puberty theme until, finally, all three scenes run again, this time in a timeframe later than the original scene(s)

This time, however, we dream, hope, wish, and sometimes achieve a final scene where all three scenes can interact. What that means is that in the third go around, I might step out with my girlfriend, walking home after (finally) achieving that kiss, and somehow the characters from the second scene will find an excuse to enter our scene, in their characters, and interact with us. And then the same thing will happen with the third scene people, who join all of the people from the first two scenes in one big happy Harold family.

Then to draw the whole thing to a conclusion we sing a song or do a group poem or something to provide closure to this long scene/game project. When it's done well it's a fascinating collage of experiences, scenes and improv games that add up to a satisfying whole.

To do it well you need some pretty sophisticated players with lots of experience working together, or you need to hold their hands a bit until they get there.

Here are some of the simple things that you will need to establish in order to get your people to the place where they can do this at all:

Editing: You will need to train your players to cut off other scenes or games that have run their course. This is called editing. You can edit another scene by simply walking in front of it and starting something new, or you can actually step out onstage and say something like "swoosh" as you bring in some new game or scene.

Of course no game can be edited or concluded unless the active players give in to the edit. This is an extension of the basic improv skill that we have called

Give and Take. By this point in the lifecycle of your troupe, players should know to chill out what they are doing and give focus to any new initiative that is coming onstage. Once the onstage players determine that the new player isn't entering their scene to **Rescue** it or add to it, they should fade off to the back of the stage.

This requires that they keep listening even when they are performing with great focus and intensity. A famous game that pre-trains your players for both editing and fading out is Freeze and Switch. Freeze and Switch enables your players to stay alert for the moments when those onstage need to be relieved from a dying scene, and keeps the onstage players alert to being relieved from performance duty.

Cheats: If you are going to perform this macroscopic game form, you are relying on your players' ability to think of some game to throw into the mix on the spur of the moment while they are onstage and twenty different things are happening. Normally they have been experiencing assigned improv games spoon-fed to them by the structure of a show, and now you want them to think of one on their own in the middle of the stage with an audience staring at them.

For an experienced player who is familiar with a large number of games, this may be no problem. But for the rest of the world, it will be a while before they can function at this level of competence and levelheaded ness. So, I would suggest that you go ahead and pre-plan a number of improv games that will be introduced in the context of the Harold, and assign them to individual players.

Then each player will go into the Harold knowing that one of their assignments, at some point in the evening, will be to edit a scene or some other game by bring their assigned game into play.

This requires that they play the role of the emcee in introducing the game, getting suggestions, etc. In order to train them for this, I acquaint them fairly early in their training with the idea that they should also learn to play the role of the emcee in every performance game. To do that I simply ask them to watch what I do in setting up the games, getting suggestions, etc., and when some other troupe members are learning the game itself I'll have them practice being the emcee. The emcee plays a crucial role in starting and stopping the game, and has, in many games, as strong a role as the actual game players.

Of course, in the Harold we are hoping that the player/emcee will only have to set up the game and that some other player/emcee will conclude the game by editing it with a new game or a scene.

You can see how this format can be a fairly demanding one, and not really accessible to total beginners. However, a good group with strong communication and listening skills and a commitment to each other can certainly get this form going and perform a complete Harold in front of a paying audience.

Paul Johan Stokstad

The Harold is satisfying not only due to the richness of its structure and the amazement of seeing so many games and scenes on a particular topic, but also due to the possibility that actual life experiences and deep feelings of the players will be represented and explored onstage. There is nothing keeping the scenes from being extremely heartfelt or even dramatic.

This offers the possibility that a half hour improvised show could include ideas and insights that will astound players and audience alike. This really is the Holy Grail of the long format crowd, doing significant, meaningful theatre, and doing it out of nothing, right away.

To do that you will need to train your players and your audiences in the possibilities of doing real scenes that have substance and truth in them. Truth onstage is deeply loved by everyone from Stanislavski to Meisner. Improv is normally considered a comic medium, so if you get to the real stuff, you've done something noteworthy. The audiences may still laugh, but it might just be because they would rather do that than cry, and in any case, at least they are feeling something.

More on getting to the deep stuff later.

There are many other elements that can be added to the Harold, especially during the opening, such as **Object Invocation** and **Rant**, not to mention **Song Challenge**(s) during the scene work. You can always add that stuff in later if you survive the first go-around. Best of luck.

Chapter 15

Contact Improv

This subject, like musical improv and long format, could easily form the subject of another entire book. Even so, we can take a quick look at it to give a flavor of the genre and consider ways in which at least preliminary elements could be incorporated into your fledgling troupe. In doing this we are simply hoping to come up with another one of many possible performance skill sets that it would be great for your people to have in their bag of tricks. Other tools might include ballet, modern and jazz dance training, mime, voice coaching, Meisner acting training, circus training, juggling, puppetry, using masks, etc. There is simply no end to the factors that could be added to the mix. Even so, contact improv is possibly the next best skillset candidate in line.

Contact improv is more typically thought of in the context of dance. It is far more likely that a dancer will have heard of or have experimented with contact improv than someone who has been trained at Second City. Even so, contact improv can significantly enrich the kind of improv that we're looking at in this book, so it will be useful to check out some of the major elements.

The overall outcome of this kind of work will be a group that is far more comfortable working with each other physically. Theatre is very physical. Improv theatre is no different. Once your players have run through even the most basic exercises of contact improv they will have experienced physical connection and trust that is far beyond our earlier trust exercises, and also far beyond what they will probably get into onstage. We can incorporate some of the extreme contact improv work into regular improv scenarios, but we'll get to that.

One thing before we jump in: this stuff is not for the shy. If you are working with a group of young players who have never been in close physical contact with other people, it may be that you can skip this whole chapter, because this stuff could overload their circuits. For everyone else, it's just powerful stuff.

To start with, you need to establish some trust. Previously we worked on developing trust in a circle, with people using their hands to support a center player that was "falling," eyes closed, toward the outer perimeter of the circle. In contact improv work we can take this up a level by having the players in the circle use other parts of their body to support the inner player. In other words, the circle players will keep the inner player safe, supporting their leaning body from falling, but using, say, their back, a shoulder, a hip or even their head to keep them in the circle. Not that the use of hands is outlawed, just that a new emphasis on the body arises.

Having tried that all around, you can move

toward a body mapping exploration, where groups of two or three partner off with one player lying face down on the ground. The other player(s) then explore the contours of the prone player's body with parts of their own body. For example, the "up" players might use a leg to touch or define the shape of the outer side of the down players torso. Maybe a head could be stuck into the back of the down player's neck. Hands could "define" the shape of an ankle.

By doing this both the up and the down players gain familiarity with exploring other people's body contours in a careful and respectful way. This builds trust and a base for exploration of sharing weight and other contact improv tools.

The next step might be to do something called "small dance." In this exercise, individuals stand by themselves and take a deep breath through the nose and then exhale through the mouth, which has a relaxing quality. Then they draw their attention to the tiny fluctuations of muscle tension that are necessary to keep their body erect. They can start by noting these fluctuations in their feet.

Having done that they can take the same in- breath and exhale, and then examine the movement of other parts of the body in space based on these tiny fluctuations. For example, it may be possible to think of the head as a kind of giant magic marker, and imagine that it is creating tiny scribbles or doodles in the air based on the muscular adjustments that we described earlier. This same imaginary visualization can be done in relation to the shoulders, the fingertips, a spot just below the navel, and the knees, with the in-breath/out-breath punctuation between each exploration.

Then the players can put their attention on the entire body as a set of tiny movements in space. Having done this, they have taken their attention to a microscopic level of their own body's functioning, which creates a basis for getting in tune with their own creative impulses.

Then we can have them begin to exaggerate these tiny doodles, scribbles or impulses. Have them extend those movements into something big enough to cause visible movements in the body.

Having done that, we can then try some group interaction again.

The group work that builds on this "small dance" exercise again puts a player in the middle of three to five players. The central player closes their eyes and gets in touch with that small dance of their own bodily impulses. Then they start to exaggerate the impulses of what they are experiencing in their own small dance so those movements become bigger, externally visible explorations and extensions of that inner movement and rhythm.

The players surrounding the center player then begin to interact with that player by following or mapping the movement of the center player with their own hands, arms, or body. The center player will naturally find themselves being touched as they extend

Paul Johan Stokstad

their small dance. Then the outer players begin to give little suggestions or nudges to the center player, in that that they might extend a particular movement or gesture of that player even further... The center player can respond to these suggestions or not.

Finally the inner player begins to make decisions to either go with or even push off of the suggestions that are coming their way.

By this time the outer players can begin to offer other parts of their bodies as movement impulses or possible "shelves" for the inner player to roll onto or slide off. This kind of shelf work is another major aspect of contact improv. At this point the inner player could even be lifted up in the air, or slide to the floor and get back up as part of the exploration.

And then everyone can rotate in.

At this point you could switch gears and try out some body surfing. Some instructors will throw this in first thing to break down inhibitions. But it may be a little easier after all of the previous work. It's fun, but, again, not for the shy. Body surfing is done by having everyone lie down in a line, side by side, on their stomachs. Then the player on the end turns and starts to extend their arms and then their body over the group at an angle perpendicular to those players that are lying down. As the player on the end does this the whole group starts to roll away from the side that the player is on.

The effect of this is to carry the end player over

the group like a package rolling along a conveyer made up of metal rollers.

Then the next player in line turns at an angle to the group and rolls over, while the player that rolled over first finishes riding on the rolling bodies and changes to a rolling body on the end of the group.

For flow rolls you will need a fairly large room.

Another thing (back on your feet) is to experiment with "shelves," where one player will offer a back or a knee or a hip for another player to lay over and maybe slide off to the floor, etc. Creating a solid structure is necessary. Just holding out an arm typically won't do unless you are a body builder.

Having experimented with these tools (and there are many more) a small group of two or three players should be able to join each other in a group improvisation where they would all give and get impulses from each other, discover levels, shelves and rolling over and around each other in a kind of expressive tangle. Remember that players need to support each other if they are falling, even slowly, toward the ground, but that individual players need to be responsible for their own safety as well. Players need to be cautioned against restraining other players hands and feet, which may become necessary for landing safely at times.

In exploring each other's weight and movement in this highly connected way, your performers begin to have a sense of trust and a sort of intuitive physical

Paul Johan Stokstad

communication. For the audience, this sort of deep connectivity is visually and even emotionally compelling. Any sort of contact onstage, even looking at each other in the eyes, engages audience interest. This is amplified exponentially when people are grabbing on and rolling around in a mass of apparently unified, intelligent physical expression.

It's easy to see how this sort of thing would amplify your troupe's performance skills. First of all, such physical contact develops trust and understanding between your players. It takes trust to allow other people to physically handle and be in contact with your body. Some very shy or defensive people can find themselves totally enamored of the surprising degree of security and tenderness that they feel in the protection of what a few weeks before were complete strangers. The other possibility is that physically expressive people will learn patience in order allow people who are less familiar with this to emerge at their own pace.

People learn to listen, give and take physically as well as verbally.

This sort of skill lends itself toward increasing the richness and effectiveness of scenes onstage, where physical contact is often an escape out of some situation that is apparently going nowhere. Grabbing on to another player in any scene demands justi-fication, and that justification is usually something compelling to both players and audience.

Contact improv can be directly integrated into a

regular improv performance using a game such as **Freeze and Melt**, where an emcee would say "melt" and the players would do contact improv, rolling all over each other, and then the emcee would say "freeze" after which one of the players would have to justify the position that they were frozen in, and continue with a scene based on that justification until the emcee said "melt" again, after which a contact improv session would ensue, until the next freeze (etc.).

An alternate "speed melt" would be all contact improv with only justifications, no scene, i.e., "melt, " "freeze," (justify), "melt," "freeze," (justify). etc.

There may be any number of other games that could be devised based on contact improv (I just made that one up). The main point here is that by working with your players in this arena you significantly amplify their mutual trust and physical expressiveness, and open the door to some new ways to play with and for others.

The exercises in this chapter may take several sessions to complete. You may want to throw some of them in as part of a regular improv workshop, over a period of weeks. The best tack in this genre may be to bring in a trained contact improv instructor (if you can find one) and or a dance teacher who is sensitive to these concepts, and have a session or two acquainting your players with these principles. Regardless of the method of introducing the material, you can apply it, as acquired, in creating new games and deepened group connection.

Paul Johan Stokstad

Chapter 16

Keeping it Together

- ➤ Dealing with new people
- ➤ Delegation
- ➤ Politics
- ➤ Money
- ➤ The Critics
- ➤ Communications
- ➤ Arthur Deming
- ➤ Margaret Meade
- ➤ Staying happy
- ➤ The dream team

Dealing with new people

One of the biggest challenges to the stability of the group is the enthusiastic arrival of new people. It's inevitable: you put weeks and months of training into a group of players and then do one show and you are instantly deluged with people who are dying to do what your players are doing, it's their life's dream, they're in love with it, they'll do anything to get started, and by the way, when can they start and when do they get onstage?

Managing the flood of interest in improv is the basis of an entire industry of training that, for all we know, is responsible for half of the GNP of a town like Chicago, where there are several versions of 18-month long training programs in improv, long format improv, Second City skit producing improv and Second City comedy-writing improv.

But for you, the new improv troupe, the concerns are the following: How do new people fit in, as personalities, with your existing group? If there is a constant influx of new people, how does the sense of intimacy and trust get created and maintained? At what point do you decide that the group is too big and create several groups?

One solution, when you have an abundance of

Paul Johan Stokstad

applicants, is just to divide the groups based on who trained with who. That is, if you have a discrete training program of four classes followed by a plunge into performance, you just keep those groups together as teams and have them play off of and compete with each other.

Another method is to have informal/optional game play sessions where new people can be integrated in to the group, working with existing troupe members, and then slowly work their way into the regular sessions with the established players.

Some groups have actually held tryouts as their numbers diminished due to the attrition of people moving or losing interest.

The main concern is that new people get along with the existing troupe members, since any group, like any family, will have personality differences.

It's a juggling act, and you are the juggler.

Delegation

As the producer, teacher, scheduler, director, video taper, show designer, and probable emcee, you are staring the B-word in the face: burnout. Unless you can effectively train and empower others to help with what you are doing, you will quickly find that what you are doing becomes an energy sink. You will probably not make enough money to compensate you for all the time you put in, but you certainly not make enough money to justify doing it all yourself.

The thing to watch out for in the delegation world is what I call the boomerang. In the boomerang, seven to eight out of ten people that you delegated to will do their jobs. Two or three will drop the ball for some reason: going out of town, sick, quitting, flat tire, got out of work late, forgot, etc. In that case, you will usually get a breathless, apologetic phone call on your answering machine explaining the astonishingly difficult situation, plus apologies, but the bottom lie is that you have that job back, just like a boomerang.

To your delegate, they can now rest easy, since they called you, didn't they? And after all, what's one more little thing added onto your plate (at least that's how it looks to them). But what they don't know is that you were already juggling three balls, and then they called, and then someone else, and then one more at the last minute, and all of a sudden you are up to six balls. Which only the pros can do, and for a matter of seconds.

My solution for this is that when I create jobs for volunteers, they have to get their own backup for when they drop the ball. That way it never has to come back to me. Oddly, sometimes I'm even performing, so I don't want to be running the tickets, the lights and the camera at the same time. This may work for you, but the main thing is, if you can't delegate, you will always have a small project. You do need to train and inspire... but you can't do it all.

Politics

Personalities are different, by definition, and every once in a while you need to sit everyone down and make sure that they are all reasonably happy. If not, problems well up. If it is a cooperative troupe, you may have to have business meetings and vote on things. If it's your project, you need to make the chain of command clear, but leave room for people to air their thoughts and feelings.

Money

If you are producing the show, you should make some money for the thing. There are very few paid improv performers. It wouldn't hurt to direct some of that money toward dance or mime training for your players, but you have to pay for things, buy equipment, etc., so, don't be afraid to pay yourself.

The Critics

There are almost always critics in and outside of the troupe. Nothing attracts critics like drama. Your troupe members will question game choices and game assignments. Straight drama people will say that you are doing something superficial, etc. Critiques from your players will often mask uncertainties that they have about some new game or performance structure. If a scene "fails" in performance, the players will inevitably blame the game, rather than look at the ways in which they violated improv principles, even simply by expecting improv to be funny or entertaining. Usually what is a disaster one day will be a hit the next.

Players need to learn to disassociate themselves from expecting a certain result onstage, and be reminded that the entertainment of the audience is not the primary goal. The audience has accepted the risk of a less than polished show when they come to an improv performance. They won't like it if we don't play by our own rules, but they don't expect a polished show. It's the process that is fascinating, not the product.

Since we aren't producing something that claims to be perfect, we should take what we hear from the perfectionists with a grain of sugar, smile, and go on with the show. If they have a serious question, you can usually deal with it by reference to what I have just described.

Communications

What can I say? You need to check in with people and make sure that they are telling you how it's going. People have to feel like they are being heard and have a way to talk to you. Improv is all about saying yes, but that doesn't mean that in real life everybody is perfect. Feelings get hurt, and people need to work all that out.

Paul Johan Stokstad

Arthur Deming

Hindsight is 20-20. You can blow it and find out how good organizations run themselves later, or you can do it right from the start. Doing it right may require learning from Arthur Deming. Arthur was the brilliant efficiency expert that guided production in the U.S. during WWII, and then, when he visited Japan, they had the audacity to listen to him and take it seriously. This of course, resulted in tremendous success.

His systems have evolved into what is called Total Quality Management (TQM). This management technique is a major success story in many industrial and business environments, and can even be applied to an improv group since it is, after all, a group work environment, of a sort. He outlined 14 points for business success, which I have redesigned for relevance to an improv group:

1. People have to understand and experience the consistency of what you are doing and why
2. Everyone should be clear on the principles and uses of improv
3. Couch side-coaching in the interest of having more fun as a group
4. Showmanship and reliability are of equal value
5. The quality and integration of the group are

always open to enhancement
6. People should keep learning and experience teaching
7. Everyone onstage should grow toward being able to "edit" onstage, taking responsibility and leadership for the overall success of the show
8. Encourage innovation and improvisation not only in games but as a performance group
9. Everyone should share in the vision, creation of and credit for the show
10. No need to beg. Just inspire
11. The audience is there to teach us, not to approve of us. We are trying out our relationship with them, and want to optimize that exchange
12. Open the door for players to become teachers and team leaders
13. Empower for personal and performance excellence
14. Make that growth part of the structure of workshop, rehearsal and performance

The gist of all this is that your players have to feel that they are part of an artistically significant venture in which they play a valued role and have a voice in its creation.

Margaret Meade

If you were surprised seeing Arthur Deming in a theatre book (his statistics buddies are rolling over in their cubicles), it must be even more odd to see Margaret Meade. The reason she got in is due to her supposed comment that there should be an incest taboo in the workplace. This statement was not made on the basis of her famous research into South Sea cultures, but after having several disastrous marital problems with co-workers becoming husbands as replacements for current husbands.

The point here is that if you can possibly encourage your performers not to date each other, things will be a lot simpler. And the same thing goes for you, if you are training and working with people that are of an age that would normally be attractive/eligible dates for you.

It's not that falling in love with someone in the troupe is in itself difficult, (although some people might get jealous, who knows?), it's the 90% chance that performer A will eventually break up with performer B at some point and they both will have to go through the whole drama with everyone in the troupe witnessing the entire thing day after day, rehearsal after rehearsal, show after show. It can be agonizing.

Of course, it's even worse if you date somebody in the troupe. Or even worse, your co-founder, since when you break up it's like mommy and daddy divorcing, with the kids choosing sides. Not that that ever happened to anyone I know. No, no, this is just imaginary. I would never do that (again).

A word to the wise is sufficient. Anyone else should read the last few paragraphs, several times.

Staying happy

Don't forget to keep yourself happy. There are a lot of people to keep entertained in a project like this. Just make sure that you include yourself in all that. Sometimes you are hoping to inspire your players to stick with it, making no money, volunteering, week after week, and you are bending over backwards to make that easy for everyone. But don't forget, when you are up to your shoulders in alligators, that your original intention wasn't to work in the swamp at all, but to build a koi pond.

Make sure that you fulfill your goals, too. If momma ain't happy ain't nobody eatin' right.

The Dream Team

The dream team would be a nice mix of friendly, outgoing, well-adjusted, reliable people who come to rehearsals and workshops on time, never miss a show or have work or family responsibilities that take them out of town, love trying out new games, are curious about improv and how it works, have flexible bodies and bravely dive into a pig pile of people without a second thought, and are also emotionally available, intellectually and culturally alert, involved and aware of books, movies, the news, other cultures, plus equally at home with singing, all kinds of dance, plus being physically expressive and uninhibited without having a deep desire to shock people, plus, of course having money to burn and enjoying the improv activity just for the fun of it and also deeply committed to making your job as easy as possible by helping set up, clean up and close up.

In addition they would have a wealth of interesting life experiences to draw on to create a Harold or even basic scenework that is insightful, compassionate, heartfelt, and poignant. Plus having a sense of fun and playful spontaneity that guarantees a fun time for all involved.

And did I mention good-looking, or at least happy with how they look?

Paul Johan Stokstad

This of course, would be an improv group in heaven, but... a guy can dream, can't he?

Chapter 17

Nowhere to go but up

- ➢ Training others

- ➢ Improv leagues

- ➢ Live Interactive Broadcast

- ➢ Online Fame and Fortune

- ➢ Corporate services

Training others

Once you get people onstage, inevitably there will be an on rush of new people wanting to get involved. It's always a challenge, managing the new along with the established players. You always have varying degrees of knowledge to deal with. Even so, if you set up a training regimen for new people and then feed them into your performance group(s), it can work out well. One effective method is to have your experienced performers segué into becoming teachers. This increases their own commitment to improv as an object of study and can cement their relationship with you, since there will probably be some financial compensation for their teaching activities.

Improv leagues

One question that emerges is what to do with all of the new people. In a worst-case scenario, you troupe membership is so fluid that the new people are constantly replenishing the troupe. This makes it challenging to establish the knowledge base and shared, intuitive communication that characterizes a long-standing group of players. One of the Chicago long-format training facilities creates a new performing group out of every class that completes its 18-month program.

The Comedy and Theater Sports people simply form more competitive teams and pit them against each other. My thought is that this could easily be extended to a league-type situation, where a number of small teams in varying age groups could compete, almost like a volleyball, softball or soccer league.

This of course requires using a scoring or competition format. Even so, it's one way to involve large groups of people.

Live Interactive Broadcast

This has been my persistent dream for many years, which I have pursued via public access TV, demo tapes, commuting 120 miles a night to do a live show in another town (bringing 8 players with me), etc. I have always been fascinated with breaking down the wall between an on-camera show and the passive audience out there in TV viewer land. When an audience provides input into a live improv show it draws them in and gives them a sense of immediacy and involvement. That it is rarely the case in the couch potato scenario that is the legacy of most television broadcast today.

Interactive television has the potential to spread this involvement over a much wider scale, such that audiences could make scene suggestions, vote on competitions, and get deeply involved in helping create and evaluate what they are watching.

I believe that the couch potato, in most cases, would rather be a couch participant. Even something as simple as phone calls in to a live show could create that situation. You may not want to put the questions on live, of course, unless you have seven second delay capability to filter out any objectionable stuff.

Online Fame and Fortune

Since I have been active for many years in online marketing and design, naturally I have been bursting with interest in the emergence of online broadcast capabilities. It doesn't take a brilliant mind to see that an interactive environment like the web could lower the cost of broadcast and instantly get a viewing audience involved in the show.

In my dream world there are a number of competitive improv troupes in major cities that go head to head against other troupes, competing online, without ever leaving their own community. Audiences could view both troupes performing the same games and assign scores.

It's a whole business plan. The technology is available.

Then of course there's the possibility of improvising with other people using a 3-d avatar that each player controls wearing a body suit and a microphone, while viewers watch and contribute scene suggestions.

Which leads to both text and 3-d avatar improv in hundreds of game rooms where audience members queue up to become performers

And on and on. The brainstorming never stops. Now to find the investors (more shy now than they used to be).

Paul Johan Stokstad

Corporate services

A number of people have established consulting services and seminars that use improv to develop spontaneity, creativity, and team building skills in corporate settings. There's no reason that you can't supplement your income while you make the business world a more fun place to be. We may not free the working masses this way, but we can help them play well with others. There are a bunch of books on this topic out there. Search Amazon and off you go.

Chapter 18

Whither Improv?

When I started writing this book I contacted one famous improv promoter and asked him to submit a jacket comment. His response was "Why you?" In other words, he hardly knew me; I hadn't trained in his full system or with any one that he knew, so why should I write an improv book?

To me, his attitude was indicative of a trend in improv that is the opposite of what this book is about. The idea that only one set of people has all the answers or even the inside track on what constitutes the best improv, or the "real" improv, is somehow odd to me.

There are probably five or six major trends in improv today. There are the competition people (Theatre Sports, Comedy Sports). There are the "improv is cool as a developer of skit material for a revue" crowd (Second City, Saturday Night Live), and there are the three or four schools of long format improv in Chicago (Improv Olympic, et al), and in San Francisco (Bay Area Theater Sports). There is even a group in Chicago blending Meisner acting training with improv.

I love that diversity, because it shows that

improv is a tool that is still intriguing people, and they are holding it up to the light, looking at it from a number of angles, and furthering the discipline.

But the idea that one way or another is the best, or that you can't know anything unless you've done it in the big city is counterproductive. I've run into this in my performing groups as well, in that one player will say that certain players should be excluded from performing, because "they aren't very good." This idea of good versus bad in improv is a potentially pernicious reversal of what improv was originally about, which was to empower children to get onstage and release their creative energies in a natural way without concerning themselves about a viewing audience.

Looking at basketball as an analogous team activity, we don't restrict ourselves from playing basketball because Michael Jordan is so good. Jordan isn't here to stop us from being our best, turning us all into passive TV viewers. He's there to inspire us to play better. And, in the same way, just because John Wooden wrote a basketball book, it doesn't mean that Joe Highschoolcoach in Wellman, Iowa doesn't have something to say about the game.

This book concerns itself with the person who isn't going to go to Chicago and study for 18 months, hoping to become the next Robin Williams or Jim Carey (why bother, it's been done?). This book is for you to use to empower yourself and people right in your own community to experience the fun of playing and watching improv onstage.

In the same vein, I don't think that anyone owns improv any more than you. Anyone who plays improv for a few weeks can think up a new improv game, and then another and another.

The idea of newer and fresher forms of improv coming up from all over the planet sounds great to me.

Here's my latest, for example:

Most current acting training tries to fully engage the individual in the moment, bringing an honesty and freshness to each performance. The Meisner technique uses a series of mirrored speech activities to achieve emotional honesty. Strasbourg training allows an individual to summon up flavors of character from within, based on a sort of invocation of experiences from the past. Other techniques use a concept of body center or psychological gesture, hoping to give actors a key to unlocking what's inside and then using that to fill out a character. The point of all these techniques is to summon energy into a character that is, otherwise, likely to be just a rote performance.

In a completely separate world of exploration, psychologists have recently discovered that there seem to be physiological correlates to emotional states. That is, for example, if you are upset about something, if you lie down, close your eyes and put your attention on your body, you will almost inevitably find that some area of your body is tingling or aching or vibrating in some way.

These psychologists postulate that that area of the body is somehow the storage area for some past experience that has a resonance with what you are currently getting upset about.

They say that your experience of something wrong in your life is probably accurate, but the charged energy surrounding the experience is due to the previous, unresolved experience. That means is that you are probably overreacting to the new trauma, which has triggered the memory (stored in a physical way) of the old one.

The technique that grows out of this research is called "focusing," which allows the user to focus on these charged physical sensations, release that trapped or blocked area, and move into life without a lot of triggers waiting to get tripped.

The point of all this for improv is that we can use a truncated version of the focusing technique to instantly achieve deep honesty onstage, and create the live, vital improv moment that is the holy grail of every serious improv player.

The way you could do this in an improv performance game would be to face away from the audience, close the eyes, and find the sensations that predominate in your body. Once you have made that inner contact, you take that feeling and extrapolate it into a single whole body gesture, possibly with a sound element, as you turn to face the audience. Then your partner onstage does the same thing. From out of that freeze you both start an improv scene or game.

Paul Johan Stokstad

Having prepared in this way, you have come in contact with exactly how you are feeling inside, and then you immediately step into performance, which then gets powerfully imbued with the authenticity of where you are in that moment.

A scene started in this way can have deeply palpable sincerity and truth. Exactly what the most serious actor works for and dreams about.

So, there you have it, a fundamentally new acting and improv performance technique from an improv coach in a small town in Southeast Iowa. We'll call it **"authentic grunt."**

The point is that you don't have to be famous to bring something to the improv table. This book is not about getting you to admire the brilliant improv experts in Chicago or any other community. It's about empowering you and your people to let out the inner brilliance that shines in every player and in you as an improv teacher, coach and producer.

Have fun.

Remember to play.

And when you are up to your %#@ in alligators, whatever happens, say yes.

Appendix A

List of workshop/skill building games described in the book and their locations in the book, by chapter:

Make Statements - 2
Mirror - 4
    ☐ Verbal- 5
    ☐ Three-peat -5
Object - 5
    ☐ Add
    ☐ 3 objects
Ooga booga - 4
Phone bank - 3
Rooms - 6
    ☐ Last
    ☐ Next
Say Yes - 2
Space Substance - 2
Stage Picture - 2
Story Circle - 5
Three Part Scene - 6
Three Statements - 3
Tiny Objects - 3
Trust - 4
    ☐ fall
    ☐ walk
Yes And… - 3

Appendix B

This is a description of games not explained elsewhere in the book and suggestions for performance staging (if applicable). This is by no means a comprehensive list, since there must be thousands of improv games out there, but this is a strong core group from which general improv staging principles could be extracted and applied to almost any game situation.

- Audience member
- By the music
- Chameleons
- Dream In the Life
- Dubbing
- Entrances & Exits
- Expert endowment
- Foreign Expert
- Foreign Poet
- Gemini
- Genre storyline
- Hitchhikers
- It's Tuesday
- Machine for performance
- Mr. Know it all
- Ms. Ask A Lot
- Object Invocation
- Park Bench
- Pigpile Machine

- Playbook
- Rant
- Rescue
- Clump Speak
- Scene from Nothing
- Screenwriter
- Shrinking and growing
- Slide show
- Song Challenge(s)
- Sportscasters
- Spotlight sing
- The Movers
- 3-2-1

Audience Member

This game is a normal improv scene, but it involves an audience member/volunteer as one of the players. They can say any of the following lines at any time in the scene that it is appropriate:

1. Yes
2. I'll go along with that
3. That works for me!

Staging Suggestions:

It's best if you prepare a card with the three statements written on it for the audience member to use as a reference point during the scene. The trained players do a regular scene, based on location and relationship suggestions from the audience, and try to involve the audience member in the action. Since the audience member can only say yes to any initiative they are instantly reasonably good improv participants. The audience member should not be mistreated in any way. Usually it will be a lot of fun for them and the audience, which will appreciate having one of their own onstage.

By the Music

This is a silent scene that takes its energy and "flavor" from the background music that is being played. By changing the background music, the pianist changes the mood and pace of the onstage activity.

Staging Suggestions:

The emcee should get a suggestion for an everyday activity for the players. It's not necessary for a big story to develop, but little initiatives and character relationships will naturally develop as the players explore the concept, discover objects in the area, etc. This has the flavor of a dance, in that the players respond to the music appropriately. The pianist/musician should look for clear, dramatic contrasts in musical genre that will lend themselves to obvious changes in onstage behavior. This can also be done with taped music, if you can't get it live.

Chameleons

In this game two players get a beginning and ending situation from the audience. Unlike most scene games, we don't worry about getting a relationship or location, since the scene will change in seconds to something new. The beginning situation is the first scene that the players start with, and the ending situation is just that. In between, the players switch from situation to situation without any visible signal between them

Staging Suggestions

This game requires extremely active listening and spatial awareness skills. Most scenes have a sort of "beat" structure, where one action leads to another. Each of these theatrical actions is traditionally called a beat. In improv, it's fairly easy to identify these beats, since, for example, two players may decide to make a phone call, but once they pick up the phone, something new is happening, i.e. - the actual call itself. That would be a new beat. In between the beats there is a kind of silence in which an improv performer would typically bring out some new initiative in the context of that situation. Rather than bringing something new out of that silence, the players in Chameleons emerge from what sometimes may even be a physical pause between beats by verbally and physically creating a new situation that justifies or explains their physical position in a new way. In essence this is a sort of freeze and switch game for two players, but it certainly has it's own fascinating character and flow from action into silence and again into action, arriving at a known conclusion which brings an audience-pleasing closure to the piece.

Dream In the Life

This game, unlike the other games in this book, is not improvised on the spot, but rather is the result of a private troupe brainstorming session, usually during an intermission. Before the break the M.C. asks for an audience member who had a particularly memorable day that day, and requests that volunteer to narrate the events of their day. After the narration, troupe members may ask questions of the volunteer in order to get more detail on the day's events.

Having gathered that info, the troupe then adjourns and maps out a short scene where they pre-enact the dream that the volunteer will have that night (after the show). After the break they come back and perform the scene. The audience enjoys the attention on one of their own.

Staging Suggestions

The brainstorming in the back room can be fast and furious... so someone has to play a guiding role to make sure that the scene has a beginning, middle and end. Slow motion and sound effects work well here, as well as a kind of dreamy collage-like logic of entering and exiting characters and appropriate sound effects. Usually one player will represent the volunteer in the scene, and having them start and end the scene lying down (or leaning on a back wall, eyes closed, for staging/visibility reasons) can serve as the opening and closing elements.

Dubbing

Dubbing typically involves four players. Two are in the scene and two are "dubbing" their voices or dialogue.

Staging Suggestions

The emcee takes location and relationship suggestions from the audience. The dubbers generally sit downstage from the players, on the opposite side of the stage from the person that they are dubbing. That enables them to see the face and mouth of the player for whom they are speaking. The challenge here is for the dubber to watch the onstage player and speak appropriately for that person's actions, and for the onstage player to make sure that they move their mouth when the dubber is speaking. If the onstage player listens carefully, he/she will be able to guess the next word that the dubber is going to use with a reasonable degree of accuracy, and so his/her mouth will move in what appears to be an appropriate fashion a high percentage of the time. Games such as mirror speech can develop some of the skills necessary to do this properly.

Entrances & Exits

The audience gives location and relationships for 3-4 players. Then the emcee asks for a word for each player that might be used in the designated location. Whenever the player's word is used in the scene they must exit or enter the scene.

Staging Suggestions

Players must justify their entrances and exits, not simply leave or show up. The scene can end with someone using their own word and sending himself or herself off stage. The emcee may need to repeat or rehearse the key words with the players and the audience a few times before the scene to make sure that they are familiar to all parties.

Expert endowment or "Meet the Expert"

This is a talk-show format where one player is sent out of the room and the audience picks some unusual expertise in which that person is an expert. Examples might be a maker of socks from vegetables, an explosives artist, or a Norwegian stump carver. Then the player is called back into the room and is interviewed by another player. The interviewee tries to guess the topic of their expertise.

Staging Suggestions:

Both players sit in chairs onstage as if they were in a TV interview show. The interviewer starts out with general questions, and gradually homes in on more and more specific topics, without giving away the actual expertise that is being discussed. The interviewee answers the questions appropriately, but without embellishing too much, since that may take them far afield of the topic of their endowed expertise. If it takes too long for the expert to make a successful guess, the interviewer starts to give bigger and bigger hints. The interviewee may guess by referring to their endowed activity in obvious terms. The audience loves having more information than the "expert."

Foreign Expert

One player speaks gibberish and the other translates into English (or whatever language you are performing in).

Staging Suggestions

The emcee plays a crucial role in "packaging" this game for the audience. She explains "we have a special guest tonight," and assigns a gibberish / nonsense name to the Foreign Expert. She explains that the foreigner doesn't speak English, but is an expert on every other topic, and asks the audience to suggest a topic for the expert to discuss. The emcee also points out and introduces the "translator." Once the audience chooses the topic, the emcee repeats it, and then the translator "translates" the topic (in gibberish) to the expert. The expert may dialogue in gibberish back to the translator in an apparent attempt to clarify the question, and then will launch into a lecture. The translator should be animated and gesture dramatically. The translator should be more under-stated and take a background role, even though they, of course, are the one making the whole thing up. The translator gets ideas from the gestures of the speaker, and the speaker may get ideas from the translator's stuff, too. One crucial element is that the translator must listen carefully for a sort of concluding statement by the speaker. Even though the speaker can't actually conclude, of course, they can fairly clearly indicate the end of the speech with body language and tone of voice.

Foreign Poet

This game shares many elements with the previous game, but there are subtle differences in presentation.

Staging Suggestions

The emcee announces that the famous poet (give gibberish name) is here, and endows the audience with the quality of being the poet's ardent fans, saying, "so, you all know her work, so please pick the title of one of your favorites among her poems, and the translator will translate." At this point the audience makes up a title, and the translator "translates" the title to the poet, and away we go. The translator shouldn't try to rhyme. Just a free verse version of the gibberish poem will suffice. One thing that we try to do in my troupes is to amaze the audience by going for the production of a poetic statement that actually has wonderful feeling and insight.

Gemini

This is simply a story told by two people, one word at a time

Staging Suggestions

You can ask for a topic from the audience. To make it more interesting the two players can physicalize or act out the story to some degree

Genre storyline

A group of four or five players stands in a line facing the audience and another player points at them to start or continue a story from where the other players leave off. The emcee gets a story or movie genre for each player, e.g. - romance, western, science fiction, detective, horror, etc.

Staging Suggestions:

The pointer player controls the flow of the story by pointing at one player to start and then pointing to any other player to continue the story, repeating the switching between players until all genres have been represented and everyone in the group has spoken at least twice. It works well if the pointing player sits or kneels in front of the group on the floor, facing the players so that they can be seen easily. The pointer can use two hands, with a raised arm pointing at the speaker, and a lowered arm pointing at the next speaker. When the pointer wants to call a switch, he/she lowers the high arm (like a musical conductor), and raises the low arm. Speaking players should try to continue the story without repeating the last word said by the previous player, but still continuing the sentence.

Hitchhikers

Four players are given attitudes by the audience, such as grumpy, happy, silly, confused, etc., and then one player starts the scene onstage, sitting in the downstage left "driver" chair of four chairs that are arranged as if they were the four seats of a car, facing the audience. The driver starts talking in a manner consistent with his attitude, and then, one by one, stops for the other players who are hitchhiking and picks them up. As each player gets in the car, they express their attitude verbally, and then all of the other players in the car take that same that attitude towards what they say. After all four players have been added, the last player to get on asks to get out, and the scene goes back to the attitude of the third player, who then gets off, and the scene goes back to the second player's attitude, who then gets off, leaving us with a short speech by the first player, in his original attitude.

Staging Suggestions

It's great if in rehearsal the various players can learn how to mime the stop of a car by leaning forward a bit on the "stop" and then jerking back a bit as the car "takes off" again into traffic.

It's Tuesday

This scene for two or more players starts and ends with the statement "It's Tuesday." The action results from the re-use of the final word in each speech made by any player. Whatever the last word in the previous speech was, it is used as an exclamation by the next player speaking, followed by an explanation of why the word used is so important. For example:

"It's Tuesday."

"Tuesday! That's when I was supposed to get married!"

"Married? You're getting married, I wish that you had told me."

"Me! It's all me, me, me isn't it. What about my mother!"

"Mother! I left my mother at the bus station!"

"Station! I've got to get back to the TV station, my fiancé's being interviewed!

"Interviewed! No one's getting interviewed today, it's Tuesday!

This scene creates excitement and has a clear beginning and end.

Machine for Performance

To make Machine (see Appendix A) into a performance game requires some activity on the part of a narrator or emcee. The machine game is run as usual, but when everyone has joined the machine and moving and making machine-like sounds, the narrator freezes the action and steps in to explain how the machine produces the product in question. If the machine was described as a banana bread making machine, for example, the narrator would endow one of the player's activity/sound combination as being the banana peeler, one being the masher, and one pushing it into the dough, mixing, cooking, packaging, etc.

Staging Suggestions:

It may be necessary to keep the machine running but turn off the sound (have the players quit verbalizing) in order for the narrator's endowments to be clear to the audience.

Mr. Know it All

This is a fun game that works apparently like magic, but is actually quite easy to do if the players maintain certain agreements (see staging suggestions). There is one narrator and three players. The players are seated in a row, facing the audience. The players answer questions posed by the audience, each contributing one word at a time, in order, until an answer has been created.

Staging Suggestions

The players should not look at each other or appear to touch each other in any way, so that it is clear that there are no signals between them.

The narrator plays a crucial role here, in introducing the three players as if they were one entity, e.g. - Mr. Know it All or Ms. Know It All (or "The Know It All" if the group of three is a mixed group of men and women). Narrator explains that the Know it All knows everything and can answer any question. The audience poses questions and the Narrator repeats them for the audience and the Know It All. The narrator also repeats the answer for clarity, sometimes making a humorous comment of some kind about the answers (which are not always brilliant, fully grammatical, or complete).

The players should try to answer the question in as few words as possible. Yes or no or short, cryptic answers are best. If any player whose turn it is to speak feels that the last word given could possibly serve as the end of a sentence that answers the question, that player should not speak. Once or twice in a session the players should break this mold and answer in a long rambling way, just for contrast.

The narrator can play an "editing" role here if she feels that the three players have assembled a complete answer by restating the successful answer to the audience, with a sense of triumph, before another player can speak.

Ms. Ask A Lot

This is a group of three players lined up as in Mr. Know it All with the sole difference in their behavior that they come up with questions one word at a time.

Staging Suggestions

This is a companion or conclusion piece to Mr. Know It All. By adding this group of three to the first group of three you get six players onstage and the groups simply ask and answer questions of each other one or both ways. Can work well if the two groups are women vs. men

Object Invocation

This activity is usually performed at the beginning of the Harold/Long Format type of performance. It is a way to explore aspects of a particular object that may serve as later scene material.

This takes the form of a series of monologues by members of the group about a particular object chosen by the audience. The players successively describe the object, talk to it, worship it, and then "become" it. That means that for several speeches the players describe, for example, a banana, and then talk to the banana, and then speak as if worshipping the banana, and then speak from the perspective of the banana. All of this may become material for use later in various scenes within a Harold, such that the use of that object will be woven in here and there. One example would be in **Three Part Scene** (see Appendix A) where the object under exploration will be used as the instrument for resolving the scene problem in the third part of the scene.

Park Bench

The emcee gets a location for a park bench and a relationship for two players. Two other players sit, stand or kneel behind the onstage players and slide their arms under the onstage players' armpits and do their gestures in the scene.

Staging Suggestions

The onstage players should try to get their arms behind the player who is doing their arm gestures. The arms players may have trouble getting comfortable, so either having them kneel or putting the front players on high chairs may be helpful. This game is intrinsically funny, but the humor is enhanced when the arms players start toying around with the front players clothing, hair, glasses, etc. Having men behind women is visually surprising due to the ungainly size (and hair) on the male arms. The women create humor by unbuttoning the guy's shirts, messing with their hair, hiking up their pants, etc.

Pigpile Machine

This is just the machine game done from a start position that is a pile of bodies.

Staging Suggestions

This allows this workshop game to start from a position of extreme contact. As the individual machine "parts" activate, they move way from and back to the pile. This creates the integration and contact that makes machine visually compelling. Beginning players are shy to touch each other, and if they do touch, it's usually a light tap with the hands, which doesn't create a compelling visual tableau. Starting things this way is more powerful

Clump Speak

In this game the players clump together and face the audience and then start to tell a story on a topic of the audience's choosing. All of the players speak at the same time.

Staging Suggestions

A slow and careful approach to the story will usually be more successful. Sometimes if the players form a half circle and watch each other they will get more of sense of where the story is going. The story will usually unfold with a surprising degree of agreement if everyone listens and no one tries to do anything too unusual.

Playbook

One player gets to say the lines from a play and the other player gets no lines and has to make them up based on what the first player reads out of the book.

Staging Suggestions:

The emcee asks the audience to choose a number between 1 and X, where X = the number of pages in the book. The player with the book then turns to the chosen page and then moves forward in the book to the next scene for two people. The reading player reads the lines of the first person in the scene and skips the lines of the second person. The person without lines makes up their own lines. The audience makes the usual array of location and relationship choices. There are a number of scene study books on the market, such as Fifty Professional Scenes for Student Actors (Kluger, ISBN 1-56608-035-5) and Two-Character Plays for Student Actors (Mauro, ISBN 0-916260-53-4). You want to make sure that you use a two-person scene for this. This can also be done with a famous playwright, such as Shakespeare, in which case you bring a Shakespeare anthology to the show and ask the audience to choose a play and then a page number within the play. The reader must then look forward for the beginning of the next two-person scene and start the improvised scene there. One tip in using

Shakespeare in this game is to have the reading player truncate long speeches by using just the first and last sentence. Players must try to stay physical and explore the scene environment in addition to the verbal activity. The player without the book must avoid getting too specific in their responses, so that they have the flexibility to respond appropriately. In this game improv no-no behaviors like asking questions are even more dangerous than usual.

Rant

Rant is a group exercise that starts with a passionate speech by one player and builds to a group shout. This is usually performed in the context of the Harold format.

Staging Suggestions:

The players face the audience, and one player steps out of the group and excitedly discusses whatever topic is under consideration. Then another player steps forward, interrupting the first, and then gives their impassioned speech. This player is then replaced as well, and so on, until all players have spoken, and then one player steps in to join the speaker without replacing them, and then another, and another, until all players are excitedly ranting on at the same time. Then the volume goes up and just at the moment when the maximum volume is reached, they all suddenly stop. At that point the first speaker can make some final summary statement or "moral of the story" comment, and you are done.

Rescue

This scene is simply a normal scene where the offstage players can enter the scene to add elements.

Staging Suggestions:

The offstage players can enter and leave the scene. Offstage in this case may simply mean lined up along the back of the stage, waiting to enter. They can add characters or even physicalize props that they feel will be of use to the scene. This is also called "Killer/Savior" because the entering player can save the scene by adding something, or come in to kill or conclude the scene, which is of course, one way of saving it.

Scene from Nothing

Two or three players simply come onstage and start a scene with no suggestions from the audience.

Staging Suggestions

This scene should be presented to the audience as a sort of virtuoso piece. It works best later in the show, after the audience has become used to giving suggestions. The audience gives nothing in the way of suggestions/The players simply come out proceed just as they might in freeze and switch by either looking at each other and starting something or by handling some imaginary objects and taking the scene from there. If the players want to impose a 3-part scene structure on the scene it can work well.

Paul Johan Stokstad

Screenwriter

The emcee asks for a genre of screenplay (mystery, romance, western, et al.) A narrator makes up characters and situations that the other players act out. The narrator stops and starts scenes at will in order to advance the story through some crisis to a conclusion.

Staging Suggestions

The screenwriter/narrator sits on a chair on one side of the stage and mimes typing on a keyboard. The other players in the troupe, having lined up on the back wall of the stage, then step out to enact the scenes described by the screenwriter. The narrator may mention sound effects that the people not in the scenes may generate as support material.

Shrinking and Growing

This is Freeze and Switch with an expanding and contracting structure. It really should be called Growing and Shrinking, but that's okay.

Staging Suggestions:

A group of players (five is a good number) face the audience. The emcee gets an every day activity for one player. One player steps out of the group and starts performing that activity. Fairly soon an "offstage" (see above) player freezes that player and steps in to create a scene as in Freeze and Switch (see Appendix A). Then another player freezes those two but instead of switching places with one of the onstage players, he adds himself to the group and creates a new scene for three people. This scene is then frozen by a fourth person who adds herself in and creates a new scene. This continues until the last player is onstage and the scene she introduced is running. The last player then finds an excuse to leave, at which time the group reverts to the previous scene. The person who started that scene then finds an excuse to leave, and then the previous scene starts up again. The diminishing onstage group sequentially steps back through all of the scenes until the original player is left onstage performing their original activity, and that's it. This

Paul Johan Stokstad

can be modified to go in the opposite direction (a true Shrinking and Growing), where the game starts with all of the players onstage, one player finds an excuse to leave, one of the remaining members creates a new scene and then finds an excuse to leave, etc. , until only one is left, and then the second to last player freezes the scene and comes back and restarts the two person scene, followed by a freeze from the person who left when there were three people. This continues until the entire group is back onstage. Also called "Lotus."

Slide Show

The emcee gets a topic for a slide show from the audience. One character volunteers to narrate the show. The rest of the players stand in a line facing the audience and when the narrator says "First slide," they move into unusual positions and stop. The narrator then justifies that tableau of players with some description of the slide. Then the narrator says "Next slide" and continues the process, ending the game with the statement "Final slide."

Staging Suggestions:

Players should make a simple move of their entire body between slides and freeze. They should explore levels and interact by leaning or draping themselves over each other. They don't need to try to tell a story, just to make interesting shapes and positions for the speaker to justify. This is a good icebreaker game to be used early in the show.

Song Challenge(s)

In this game a scene is performed but at any time an audience member can call out "song" and the action is stopped, a genre of music is chosen, and the performers improvise a song, and then proceed with the scene. There may be one, two, three or more songs in a song challenge. One is plenty, two brave, three ambitious, and anything more is a whole musical, face it.

Musical Improv is described in some detail in Chapter 13, but a few additional comments are in order. You will want to practice several genres in workshops to the point that you feel relatively confident about doing them. A sample list might be tango, opera, rock and roll, blues, folk, reggae, and maybe even rap/hip hop. Once a new genre has been stabilized, you can add it to a list of song genres that you put on a poster on the wall on the performance night. That way, when the song challenge scene is stopped, the audience member that stopped the scene will choose a song genre with which everyone onstage has some familiarity.

Sportscasters

The audience is asked for an everyday household activity for one player. Two other players then comment on that activity as if it was a sports activity.

Staging Suggestions

The two commentators sit off to the side in two chairs. The player onstage shouldn't try to clown or dramatize their actions. This creates a contrast with the highly dramatized version of what they are doing as presented by the commentators. The commentators take the two distinct roles of "play-by-play" and color commentator, as is usually the case in a sports broadcast. The play-by-play person simply describes what is happening, and the color commentator comments on the history, technique, etc. They whole piece can be introduced as "What sportscasters do at home," or "What sportscasters do on their day off."

Paul Johan Stokstad

Spotlight Sing

This game is similar to **Rant** in that a single player emerges from a line of players in the back of the stage and starts to sing, standing in a spotlight (if available), and subsequent players push them out of the light and start to sing their own song. In this case the songs are not improvised, but are popular songs of any kind.

Staging suggestions:

Even though each subsequent player appears to be hungry for attention to the point that they are pushing the previous player off stage, they are actually doing the singer a favor by limiting the lone exposure time. It can be fascinating if the song snippet choices start to take on a theme, such as:

Tonight, Tonight (from West Side Story)
Oh What A Beautiful Morning (Oklahoma)
Tomorrow, Tomorrow, I Love Ya, Tomorrow (Annie)

The Movers

$\mathbf{T}$wo or more players get scene and relationship suggestions from the audience. Each onstage player is matched with a "mover."

Staging Suggestions

One of the movers puts a player into a position, and then that player can speak a line. Then another mover moves his player into a position to respond to the first statement. This continues for the entire scene. The movers should feel free to move the speaking players into dramatic positions. That gives the verbal players more to play with. At the same time all players remain sensitive to the needs of the scene as it unfolds.

Paul Johan Stokstad

3-2-1

This is performed with at least six people, since it involves three separate scenes. In the first scene, the players can use three word sentences, in the second, two words only, and in the last, just one word sentences.

Staging Suggestions:

Location and relationship choices are taken for each scene (just before the scene is played). Players should be patient with silence, and try to use believable phrasing, not telegram-like speech. There are many times when few words are necessary to communicate. It's really easy. Be patient. Okay?

* * * * * * * * * * * *

About the Author

Paul has started five or six (he's lost count) improv groups and has produced 75+ shows including on-camera live TV shows with remote audience input. He has trained hundreds of improv players in university, high school and private acting conservatory settings. His groups have done musical improv, contact improv, Chicago-style long format improv, dance improv, and have often generated and performed skit and song-parody material based on improv-generated ideas.

Paul is a creative and friendly type, with an extensive background in professional writing, teaching and web marketing. He has been active in advertising copywriting and print publication management for 25 years, taught ad copywriting on the graduate level for ten years, and was an early adopter of web technologies, founding a web consulting and design group in 1996. He writes poetry, essays, ad copy, movie reviews, stand-up comedy, fiction, literary journalism, a humor column, a web marketing/design column, etc. He has many interests other than improv, including tennis (he's a certified teaching pro), Transcendental Meditation, poetry writing, and performance-oriented partner dance. He consults in web marketing and design, has a website at http://www.stokstad.com and has also launched several peace-oriented websites: http://www.peacecongress.us, and http://www.peace-store.us.

Credit where it's due

No improv book should be published without some mention of Viola Spolin, who developed theatre games as a means of training children in theatre, and further developed them as a means of acting training for adults. Her work gave rise to the Compass Players, Second City, and, ultimately, Saturday Night Live, and provided a training foundation for many of the writers and performers that we enjoy today. Many of the games in this book were designed, named and described by her. You would do well to check out her many publications and teaching aids (at Northwestern University Press, or on Amazon.com)

Keith Johnstone is another foundational force in improv, both intellectually and as the originator of the Theatre Sports phenomenon. For more about him and the competition format (and much more), see improv.org.

Locally, we benefited tremendously by a musical Harold workshop provided by Charna Halpern of Chicago's Improv Olympic. Her book (mainly about long format improv) is *Truth in Comedy: The Manual of Improvisation*.

We also owe a big group hug to Anna Peterson for her inspired guidance in contact improv, and to Michael Goodman, for years of intrepid service and divine musical contributions in the oh-so-crucial arena of Musical Improv.

I welcome your thoughts, comments and questions on this book and/or on improv performance issues. I'm at paul@stokstad.com